A Short History of Economic Thought

This book, now in its third edition, provides an elementary introduction to the history of economic thought. A chapter is devoted to each of the major developments in the history of the discipline, and the concluding chapter draws together some of these key strands and comments on some major works and textbooks in the history of economic ideas. The authors also reflect on the changes in economic thinking within the general context of the philosophy of science.

This new edition continues to offer the clear and concise coverage of the main schools of thought and paradigm shifts in the field that has become the volume's trademark. The book has been thoroughly updated throughout in order to reflect changes in the landscape of the field. Details on key thinkers, and aspects such as the evolution of scholarship on growth and development, have been added or expanded, whilst not compromising on the book's concise approach. New updates include:

- Up-to-date biographical and bibliographical information.
- A discussion of the North American economists John Kenneth Galbraith and Kenneth Ewart Boulding.
- Information on developments in institutional economics, addressing in particular the works of the 2009 Nobel Prize winner Elinor Ostrom.

This book has become well known for its innovative coverage of the economic thinking of mainland Europe, whilst also addressing Anglo-American trends. It provides a short and highly readable overview of the evolution of economic thought, usable in courses where the history of economic thought constitutes only a small part of required background reading. It continues to be an extremely useful, much needed text for all introductory economics courses in the field.

Bo Sandelin is Professor of Economics at the University of Gothenburg, Sweden.

Hans-Michael Trautwein is Professor of International Economics at the University of Oldenburg, Germany.

Richard Wundrak was formerly Professor at the University of Greifswald, Germany.

A Short History of Economic Thought

Third edition

**Bo Sandelin,
Hans-Michael Trautwein
and Richard Wundrak**

Routledge
Taylor & Francis Group

LONDON AND NEW YORK

Third edition published 2014
by Routledge
2 Park Square, Milton Park, Abingdon, Oxon OX14 4RN

and by Routledge
711 Third Avenue, New York, NY 10017

Routledge is an imprint of the Taylor & Francis Group, an informa business

© 2014 Bo Sandelin, Hans-Michael Trautwein and Richard Wundrak

British Library Cataloguing in Publication Data
A catalogue record for this book is available from the British Library

Library of Congress Cataloging-in-Publication Data
Sandelin, Bo, 1942–
 A short history of economic thought / Bo Sandelin, Hans-Michael
Trautwein, and Richard Wundrak. – 3rd ed.
  pages cm
 1. Economics–History. I. Trautwein, Hans-Michael, 1957–
II. Wundrak, Richard. III. Title.
HB75.S293 2014
 330.09–dc23   2014006786

ISBN: 978-1-138-78019-4 (hbk)
ISBN: 978-1-138-78020-0 (pbk)
ISBN: 978-1-315-77089-5 (ebk)

Typeset in Times New Roman
by Swales & Willis Ltd, Exeter, Devon

Contents

Illustrations

Figures

Tables

Preface

This is an unusually small book on the history of economic thought. It is not intended to compete with the excellent, full-length books that are suitable for a full course on this subject. The purpose of this book is to provide a brief general overview, usable in courses where the history of economic thought constitutes only a small part. Evidently, teachers would often like to include such an overview in introductory economics courses, but most textbooks are too comprehensive (and expensive) for that purpose. The shortness of this book is achieved by not giving all economists who deserve it a 'fair' space, but by concentrating on a few representatives of schools and ideas. The text starts with an explanation of why it is useful to study the history of economic thought, and it ends with a short guide to those longer books for further reading.

Since 1995, our 'short history' has come out in four Swedish, one Esperanto and two English editions. This third edition has been updated and slightly revised (without making it longer). We are grateful to numerous colleagues who have helped to develop the book with their reviews and comments. In order to keep the book short, we cannot name them all, nor could we heed all their advice.

1 Introduction

Economics is a relatively young academic discipline. Until the early twentieth century, only a few chairs existed at the established universities of Europe and North America, mostly in the faculties of law or philosophy. In the turbulent period between the two World Wars, when deflation, hyperinflation and the Great Depression raged in many countries, the public interest in economics was greatly intensified. But its breakthrough as a prominent and widely studied discipline came only after the Second World War, roughly sixty years ago.

Economic thinking, on the other hand, has a much longer tradition. Early writings about markets, money and other economic issues can be found in the Bible, in ancient Greek philosophy and in medieval tracts. The rise of national states in the sixteenth to eighteenth centuries was accompanied by the propagation of trade strategies and industrial policies, some of which keep reverberating in modern debates about globalization. The century between the 1770s and the 1870s was the classical era of economic thinking, in which many of the foundations of modern economics were laid. The neoclassical view that was developed in the late nineteenth century still dominates current economic research and teaching.

With the post-war breakthrough of the discipline, however, the general mode of economic thinking began to change. As a quick glance at the leading journals and textbooks will show, economics is nowadays strongly characterized by strictly formalized reasoning in mathematical models, and by the quantification of market interaction and effects of policy measures in terms of econometrics, simulation or even experiments. Many economists tend to regard their discipline as the physics of the social sciences, striving to derive explanations of observable phenomena from a minimum set of universal principles. Designing specific policies as outcomes of their models, they also like to describe their work – half critically, half self-admiring – as 'social engineering'.

What, in such a rigorous, progress-oriented discipline, can be the use of the history of economic thinking? Isn't all that is worth knowing embodied in the present state of the art? A clear indication that history still matters to modern economists is the frequent use that they make of such labels as, say, *neo-classical, New Keynesian,* or *neo-Schumpeterian,* to mark elements of tradition in their theories. Since the labels are shorthand expressions that refer to sets of distinctive ideas and methods, which are often matters of deep and recurring controversies, it helps to have some knowledge of those earlier thinkers and schools of thought. Mostly without using the labels, modern politicians, too, refer to the ideas of older economists, rightly or wrongly. Again, evaluating the strengths and weaknesses of those ideas could help to put them in context.

The history of economic thinking may thus be used like a map or a landscape in which various schools of thought are located in different places, and where the objects of explanation form mountains, rivers, swamps and jungles between those places. The most modern, currently dominating school may be located in a prominent place, providing a clear view over large parts of the ground from a high level. But in order to gain a full view of the objects of explanation, one may have to track the ways back to older schools of thought that yield different perspectives on them. The history of economic thought may, furthermore, help to find crossroads at which alternative routes of thinking could have been (and can still be) taken. It may thus provide some orientation, not only on alternative ideas of the past, but also for promising directions of research in the future.

This short history of economic thinking is a very rough map that covers a large area by broadly outlining the main schools and tracks. We hope that it can nevertheless give the reader a fair idea of what could be found in more detailed maps. Some guidance to such finer maps will be provided, both in the references at the end of each chapter and in the final chapter, where we comment on some major works and textbooks on the history of economic ideas. In the final chapter, we will also briefly reflect on the changes in economic thinking in the more general terms of the philosophy of science. It might be argued that such methodological discussion should be at the beginning of the book, not at its end. We think, however, that we should first relate *what* economists have been thinking before we discuss *how* and *why* they changed their ideas in the course of time.

2 Pre-classical economic thought

As long as humans have lived on earth, they have resolved economic questions such as how to divide an available amount of food between consumption today and consumption tomorrow, or how to divide labour between the members of a group. Written documents of reflections on economic matters are available for a period of more than 2,000 years, beginning with the biblical writers and the ancient Greeks. More recent writers, such as the scholastics in the thirteenth century and Adam Smith in the eighteenth century, were deeply read in those ancient works. They transmitted some ideas to our time and rejected others. We begin with a few passages about the earliest manifestations of economic thinking (see Figure 1).

The ancient Greeks

Many concepts and questions that are still important in economics are found in ancient authors such as Xenophon (c. 430–c. 354 BC), Plato (427–347 BC) and Aristotle (384–322 BC). They wrote about the division of labour and specialization, money, exchange, value, self-interest, estate management and public administration. Let us see how they treated a few of those questions.

Division of labour

In *Politeia* (c. 370 BC; translation: *The Republic*) Plato described how a society develops with a division of labour that results in higher productivity:

> 'Well,' I said, 'a community starts to be formed, I suppose, when individual human beings find that they aren't self-sufficient, but that each of them has plenty of requirements which he can't fulfil on his own. Do you have an alternative suggestion as to why communities are founded?'

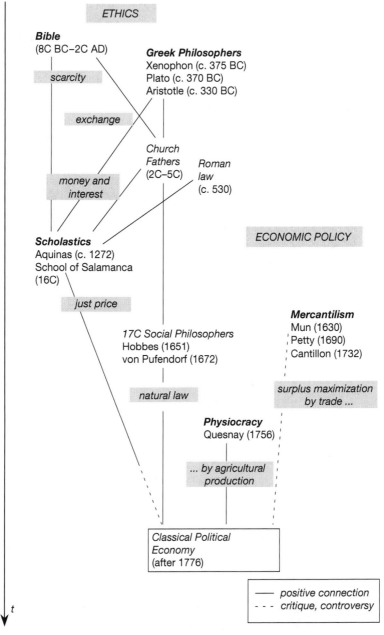

Figure 1 Pre-classical economic thought

'No,' he said.

'So people become involved with various other people to fulfil various needs, and we have lots of needs, so we gather lots of people together and get them to live in a single district as our associates and assistants. And then we call this living together a community. Is that right?'

'Yes.'

'And people trade goods with one another, because they think they'll be better off if each gives or receives something in exchange, don't they?'

'Yes.'

'All right, then,' I said. 'Let's construct our theoretical community from scratch. Apparently, its cause is our neediness.'

'Of course.'

'And the most basic and most important of our needs is that we are provided with enough food for existence and for life.'

'Absolutely.'

'The second most important is our need for somewhere to live, and the third is our need for clothing and so on.'

'True.'

'All right,' I said. 'How will our community cope with all this provisioning? Mustn't one member of it be a farmer, another a builder, and another a weaver? Is that all the people we need to look after our bodily needs? Shall we add a shoemaker to it as well?'

'Yes.'

'And there we had our community. Reduced to its bare essentials, it would consist of four or five people.'

'So it seems.'

(Plato 1993, pp. 369–70)

Plato then went on to introduce more and more specialized tasks in a larger and larger society. The economic message was that efficiency increases if everyone can specialize in the tasks for which she or he is best qualified. Specialization is also discussed in Xenophon's *Cyropaedia* (c. 375 BC). Xenophon argued that in small towns one person may produce furniture, doors, ploughs, and perhaps complete houses. In large cities, in contrast, a craftsman may specialize and become more skilful at one of these things. More than two thousand years later, we find the same discussion in Adam Smith, with the same kind of craftsmen.

Exchange, money and interest

In his *Politics* and *Ethics* (c. 330 BC) Aristotle treated economic questions such as exchange, money, prices and value. Although he may have intended to be analytical, it is the moral undertones that are most striking. Aristotle's interest in exchange presupposes private ownership, which he deemed to be good because it increases efficiency, whereas Plato was more inclined to support collective ownership. Aristotle considered the exchange of one commodity for another to be natural. Such an exchange is subject to limitations because human needs are limited. If one gets an extremely large quantity of a thing, it may be harmful or at any rate not be useful. This was Aristotle's way of saying what Adam Smith in the eighteenth century expressed by writing that 'the desire of food is limited in every man by the narrow capacity of the human stomach'. The same idea returned in neoclassical thought at the end of the nineteenth century, in the concept of diminishing marginal utility.

Exchange involving money is not natural, but to sell in order to acquire money to be able to buy another good is, nevertheless, a necessary form of exchange. Usury, i.e. money lending in order to get interest, is a perverted form of exchange. It is natural that crops and cattle multiply, but not money; money is created in order to be a medium of exchange. This negative view of interest-taking persisted for a long time. It can be found in the medieval scholastics, and it was firmly held within the Catholic Church. Regarded as usury, interest was forbidden or regulated by usury laws, of which remnants still exist in many countries. This negative view on interest is found today in Islamic thought, and there are also secular organizations working for an interest-free economy.

Value and prices

Aristotle used a distinction that can also be found more than 2,000 years later in the classical economists and especially in Marx, namely the distinction between value in use and value in exchange. Aristotle used a shoe as an example. A shoe can be used as footwear; then it has a use value. However, it can also be sold or exchanged for another good; then it has a value in exchange. In this context, Aristotle touched upon the concept of the *just price* in exchange, a concept that the medieval scholastics came to develop further (see below).

The Bible

Although the Bible is not primarily a book on economics, there are economic features within it. Some of these are similar to those found in the works of the Greek philosophers, especially with regard to interest-taking. At least in the Old Testament, the basic attitude towards interest is negative. 'You shall not charge interest on anything you lend to a fellow countryman, money or food or anything else on which interest can be charged' (Deuteronomy 23:19). In the New Testament there is no such attitude.

The problem of scarcity is the central economic problem. It arises after the Fall of Man, and is resolved in various ways in the Bible, not only by hard work. One way is by *faith*. During the Exodus, Moses asks God what to do when the people are dissatisfied because of a lack of water. God tells him to strike the rock with his stick. Moses does so; he believes they will be sustained by water from the rock, and this indeed is what happens (Exodus 17). Another solution, closely related to the first, is to *set one's mind on God's kingdom*. Let us look at an example from the New Testament:

> . . . do not ask anxiously, What are we to eat? What are we to drink? What shall we wear? All these are things for the heathen to run after, not for you, because your heavenly Father knows that you need them all. Set your mind on God's kingdom and his justice before everything else, and the rest will come to you as well.
>
> (Matthew 6:31–3)

A third solution is by *observance of the law*:

> You are to observe these commandments, statutes, and laws which I give you this day, and keep them. If you listen to these laws and are careful to observe them, then the LORD your God will observe the sworn covenant he made with your forefathers and will keep faith with you. He will love you, bless you and cause you to increase. He will bless the fruit of your body and the fruit of your land, your corn and new wine and oil, the offspring of your herds, and of your lambing flocks, in the land which he swore to your forefathers to give you.
>
> (Deuteronomy 7:11–13)

The scholastics

Scholastic thought is sometimes considered as an amalgamation of three different intellectual traditions. One is Aristotle's philosophy, another is the Bible and the Church Fathers, and the third is Roman law. The heyday of scholasticism was the thirteenth and fourteenth centuries, and Thomas Aquinas (1225–74) is its main representative. The rise and decline of the School of Salamanca in the sixteenth century marks the end of the scholastic era. The scholastics were theologians and philosophers, and it was as such that they made statements on economic matters. They expressed opinions on the just price, the rate of interest and natural law.

The just price and interest

According to the schoolmen, the *just price*, already discussed by Aristotle, is the price that would appear spontaneously on the market if nobody was deceived, or exerted coercion against anybody else, and if the situation was also normal in other respects. Consequently, the price on a monopoly market is not just.

The attitude towards the just price determined the view on interest-taking. Basically, the scholastics were against interest-taking, like Aristotle, the early biblical authors and the Church Fathers. As money was seen as a mere medium of exchange, it was considered unnatural and greedy to try to make money multiply. However, several scholastic authors presented exceptions where interest is permitted. For instance, if the borrower does not repay his debt in due time, the lender may claim interest on the overdue payment. Other authors argued that if the lender can show that the loans give rise to costs, perhaps even in the form of lost profits, he may claim compensation.

Natural law

An important concept in scholastic thinking is *natural law*. On a general level, natural law can be defined as a system of moral principles found in the order of things and in the nature of man, independent of any legislative body. For Thomas Aquinas, natural law is that part of the eternal law of God which is knowable by humans by means of their powers of reason. The idea of natural law was present already in ancient Greek philosophy, but the schoolmen treated it in greater detail, attempting to draw dividing lines between divine design and human conventions. They influenced, in turn, the social philosophers of the seventeenth century, such as Hugo Grotius (1583–1645), Thomas Hobbes (1588–1679) and Samuel von Pufendorf (1632–94), who regarded society as being established on contract by individual wills and discussed the relationship between civil rights, in particular private property, and the power of the state. Part of the social philosophy of natural law was adopted by Adam Smith and other classical economists. It can be perceived behind much of today's economic reasoning, too.

More ethics than analysis

We may summarize economic thought from the ancient Greeks to the scholastics by stating that it is mostly normative, about ethics and justice rather than about the causes and effects of the economic phenomena in question. The discussion was connected with trade or other forms of exchange, attempting to bring private ownership and the accumulation of money into line with the communal and religious norms of Antiquity and the Middle Ages. Production was of minor importance, but as we found in Plato's and Xenophon's treatment of the division of labour, it was not completely neglected.

Mercantilism

The form of economic thinking that predominated during the rise of modern nation states, between the sixteenth and eighteenth centuries, came to be known as mercantilism, mostly through the sharp criticism levelled at it by Adam Smith in his *Wealth of Nations* (1776). The origin of the name (*système mercantile*) is credited to the French physiocrat Marquis de Mirabeau (1715–89). It refers to the central policy prescription that the state should act like a merchant, augmenting the wealth of the nation by maximizing the surplus from trade with other nations. Mercantilism was not a coherent school in the same way as scholasticism in the thirteenth century, but it contains some unifying features such as interest in the balance of trade and in economic growth. Some national differences can nevertheless be discerned in terms of emphasis. German authors often wrote about public finance; their version of mercantilism is sometimes called *cameralism*. In French mercantilism, the question of how to support and govern domestic industries was important, especially when Jean-Baptiste Colbert (1619–83) had a leading influence on economic policy. Spanish mercantilists directed their attention to the questions of how to acquire precious metals and how to obtain a trade surplus. The balance of payments was also of central importance for British and Dutch mercantilists. Mercantilism meant a shift in focus from ethics and justice to production, growth and wealth.

The government and the mercantilist system

Culturally, Europe was largely unified during the Middle Ages by the Roman Catholic Church and the Latin language, which was spoken at all universities. The situation was different in economic and political respects. What we now know as countries were long divided into many, more or less independent units with local rulers who claimed tolls. To give an example, a merchant who travelled on the Rhine from Basle to Cologne at the end of the sixteenth century had to pay a toll at thirty-one different points – roughly every fifteen kilometres. Mercantilism worked against such fragmentation and for centralization. The state should consist of a unified territory, often defined as a nation.

What role should the government have in the economy? Mercantilist thought implies that the economy should be governed in such a way as to strengthen the power of the state relative to other nations. This is often regarded as the most important goal. Another goal is wealth, especially the wealth of the sovereign and the commercial elite. The following sections relate to factors underlying the power and wealth of the state.

Trade and protectionism

Trade is desirable in the opinion of mercantilism, especially trade with other countries. Trade creates wealth in terms of an inflow of money. Exports should, with a few exceptions, be promoted. Imports of goods might be accepted in payment for the country's exports, but it would be better to be paid in gold and silver. Imports are to be kept at a low level by different kinds of tariffs and regulations, aimed at securing a surplus in the trade balance, i.e. an excess of exports over imports. The Englishman Thomas Mun (1571–1641) expressed himself in the following way in a well-known book, entitled *England's Treasure by Forraign Trade* (1630): 'The ordinary means therefore to increase our wealth and treasure is by Forraign Trade, wherein we must ever observe this rule, to sell more to strangers yearly than we consume of theirs in value'.

As it was considered more important to sell than to buy, mercantilism is sometimes said to be characterized by a 'fear of goods'. This is well captured by an expression used by French mercantilists: *décharger le royaume de ses marchandises* – to unburden the kingdom of its goods. Various different factors lay behind such an attitude. One is the primitive idea, criticized by Adam Smith, that the wealth of the nation consists of its money, gold and silver, and that it should be increased by net exports. Another factor was the idea that if imports were restricted, domestic producers would be encouraged to replace them. Such import substitution (or, alternatively, export subsidies) would help to employ idle resources and increase the wealth of the nation. Many of those mercantilist views are still popular today in the management literature and policy debates about the 'competitiveness' of the national economy – debates in which international trade is essentially regarded as a zero-sum game about market shares and jobs, where one country loses what another country gains.

Views on exports and imports changed towards the end of the mercantilist era. In the eighteenth century, several authors wrote about the reciprocal advantages of international trade, i.e. imports could also be useful. In the background one can discern thoughts about the international division of labour as well as reflections on the 'unnaturalness' and impossibility of the idea that all should only sell.

Money

Money takes a central position in mercantilist thought, even if the attitude was not as narrow-minded as presented by Adam Smith. The view of money was closely bound up with the protection of domestic production. Mercantilist authors were generally aware of the main elements of what is nowadays known as the quantity theory of money. They realized that an inflow of money and precious metals, i.e. an increase in the volume of means of payment due to a trade surplus, could inflate prices in the country. However, even if people complain about higher prices, mercantilist authors argued that inflation stimulates trade, production and employment. For this to occur, though, it is necessary that money is not hoarded but circulated in the economy.

The idea that the wealth of a nation is measured by its amount of money and precious metals can be found in less sophisticated mercantilists, but it is easy to find more elaborate ideas. For instance, the Englishman William Petty (1623–87), the 'father of political arithmetic', made detailed calculations of the wealth of England and Wales in about 1665. He included real property and personal property, and even a value for the population. Money represented only a few per cent of the national wealth. A few decades later, Charles Davenant (1656–1714), an English mercantilist, argued that successful export policies require the abolition of import restrictions; he is hence often considered a precursor of economic liberalism. He published various pamphlets that give a detailed analysis of the balance of trade and of the national wealth, in which durable goods play an important role.

Towards the end of the mercantilist period, several scholars published important contributions that are even less clearly within a certain school. The Scot John Law (1671–1729), the creator of one of the first big speculative bubbles, wrote on the theory of value, giving scarcity a prominent role, and on the supply of money through the creation of credit. Richard Cantillon (c. 1680–1734), of Irish origin and living in France, was one of the few who succeeded in making a fortune from Law's financial schemes. He is sometimes considered a mercantilist, sometimes a forerunner of physiocracy, or of classical and even neoclassical economic analysis. An original thinker of his own making, he developed the concept of the economy as a two-sector system of flows of income that is balanced by market forces of supply and demand. The Italian Ferdinando Galiani (1728–87) made important contributions to systematic balance-of-payments analysis and theories of value based on both utility and scarcity. He was one of the strongest critics of the physiocratic school that came to flourish in the middle of the eighteenth century.

Physiocracy

France was the centre of physiocracy. The beginnings of the school are generally dated to 1756 when its main figures François Quesnay (1694–1774) and Anne Robert Jacques Turgot (1727–81) made their first contributions. The end is often associated with the publication of *De l'intérêt social* by Guillaume François Le Trosne (1712–80) in 1777. Physiocracy may be regarded both as a reaction against mercantilism and as a manifestation of the agromania that prevailed in Europe in the eighteenth century. The word *physiocracy* is of Greek origin and means 'power of nature', which is an indication of the views of the physiocrats. *Les économistes* was the term that the representatives of the group used to denote themselves. The group is often considered the first real school in economic thinking, with a journal of its own and regular meetings. Sometimes the physiocrats have even been regarded as a sect, because they were so tightly linked to their leader Quesnay.

Natural order

The physiocrats believed in a *natural order* of nature and society. Here, we discern elements of the philosophy of natural law. Because of bad laws, the actual order of society may differ from the natural order. Among the shortcomings are mercantilistic features such as support for industry and exports at the expense of agriculture and consumption. The bad laws should be abolished and the natural order should be restored. Private ownership was seen as an integral part of the natural order, required to encourage the work necessary for the prosperity of society.

When the natural order prevails, there is harmony between different interests. 'The whole magic of a well-ordered society', said Quesnay, 'is that each man works for others, while believing that he is working for himself'. This idea recurs in Adam Smith's famous metaphor of the invisible hand of markets, and it is a key element of economic liberalism.

Only agriculture yields a net product

Agriculture had a central position in physiocratic thought. It was argued that agriculture is the only industry that can yield a net product, a surplus over and above the costs of production. Elements of this idea are present in late mercantilist literature, too. However, the physiocrats emphasized that a prerequisite for the positive net result is that agriculture has sufficient real capital such as draught animals, cattle and tools. This makes it possible to obtain harvests sufficient not only for seed and to feed the leaseholder's family and employees, but also to feed a class of landlords.

According to the physiocrats, the capacity of agriculture to yield a net product had been counteracted by mercantilistic policies. Agriculture should be restored to its full prosperity. However, when this goal has been reached, further growth is not to be expected. While agriculture yields a net product, trade and manufacturing are sterile in the sense that the product is not worth more than the costs of production. Consequently, government taxes should be taken from the surplus of agriculture, that is, from the rent that the landlords receive.

Tableau économique

Quesnay's *Tableau économique* is probably the best known heritage left by the physiocrats. The table, published in several versions, has been regarded as a forerunner of Marx's schemes of reproduction, input–output analysis, modern national accounting systems, multiplier analysis and general equilibrium analysis. A slightly modified version of Quesnay's table illustrates the similarity to an input–output table (see Table 1).

The society consists of three classes: the productive farmers (who do not own the land), the landlords, and the sterile class (i.e. those engaged in trade and manufacturing). The table shows the flows of goods between the classes, represented by the equivalent flows of money in the opposite direction (as payments in market exchange). Thus, we find that the landlords as consumers spend 2 billion *livres* (units of money) on goods, half of which come from the productive farmers and the sterile class, respectively. Total production in the economy is as large as total consumption, i.e. 7 billion *livres*. The sterile class consumes exactly as much as it produces, i.e. 2 billion *livres*. That is why it is considered sterile. The productive class, in contrast, produces an equivalent of 5 billion *livres* but consumes only 3. The landlords produce nothing, but consume 2 billion *livres*, which is equivalent to the net product of the productive farmers. The transfer of rent, i.e. the net product of 2 billion *livres*, from the farmers to the landlords, is not apparent in the table, but it is of course required to make the flows of income and expenditure consistent with each other.

Quesnay's *Tableau économique* illustrates that economists had now begun to study the relationships between the different parts of the economy systematically. It contains the idea of the economy as a circular flow of goods and money on the analogy of the circulation of blood, reminding us of the fact

Table 1 Quesnay's *Tableau économique* (simplified)

	Consumers Productive	Landlords	Sterile	*Total Production*
Producers				
Productive	2	1	2	5
Landlords	–	–	–	–
Sterile	1	1	–	2
Total Consumption	3	2	2	7

that Quesnay was originally a physician. In different structures, modern economics still uses the representation of the economy as a circular flow of income and expenditure as a powerful tool of analysis.

References

Aristotle (1972) Politics, in *Aristotle in Twenty-Three Volumes*, XXI. London: Heinemann.

Heckscher, Eli F. (1935, reprinted 1994) *Mercantilism*. London: Routledge.

Herlitz, Lars (1989) *Ideas of Capital and Development in Pre-classical Economic Thought: Two Essays*. Institute of Economic History, University of Göteborg, Report 7.

Lowry, S. Todd (ed.) (1986) *Pre-classical Economic Thought*. Boston, Dordrecht, Lancaster: Kluwer Academic Publishers.

Magnusson, Lars (1994) *Mercantilism: The Shaping of an Economic Language*. London: Routledge.

Plato (1993) *Republic*, translation Robin Waterfield. Oxford: Oxford University Press.

Schumpeter, Joseph A. (1954) *History of Economic Analysis*. Oxford: Oxford University Press, Part II.

Vaggi, Gianni (1987) *The Economics of François Quesnay*. London: Macmillan.

3 Classical political economy

The Scottish philosopher Adam Smith (1723–90) is generally considered to be the founder of the classical school in economics. His famous *Inquiry into the Nature and Causes of the Wealth of Nations* was published in 1776, and we may regard this year as the beginning of the classical period, which lasted about one hundred years. The Irishman John Elliot Cairnes (1823–75) is sometimes regarded as the last important classical writer, publishing his *Leading Principles of Political Economy Newly Expounded* in 1874. Between them we find as main figures the Frenchman Jean-Baptiste Say (1767–1832) and the Britons Thomas Robert Malthus (1766–1834), David Ricardo (1772–1823), Nassau William Senior (1790–1864), James Mill (1773–1836) and his son John Stuart Mill (1806–73). We also find the German Karl Marx (1818–83), the famous critic of classical political economy, who nevertheless used the analytical tools of the classical school (see Figure 2).

Some characteristics are common to most classical economists. One is the interest in growth and development, which they usually thought would culminate in a stationary state, in which the economy would just reproduce itself – 'zero growth' in modern terms. Another characteristic is the concentration on the cost of production as the main determinant of prices. A third characteristic is the concern about the distribution of income between labour, land and capital in the form of wages, rents and profits. Combining all three characteristics, the classical economists attempted to provide a consistent explanation of the changing relations between income distribution and prices in the course of economic development. They developed principles of economic analysis from which the prescriptions for economic policy could be logically deduced. Nearly all of their major works carried the words *Principles of Political Economy* (Malthus, Ricardo, John Stuart Mill) or at least *political economy* in their titles (Say, Senior, James Mill, Marx and others). Most classical economists argued that the system of markets is a self-stabilizing mechanism of distribution that works efficiently without much government intervention. This idea was present in physiocratic and late mercantilist thought, too. In the main, however, mercantilists advocated far-reaching government intervention, and thus became the main target of critique by Smith.

In this chapter, we devote most of the space to Smith and his *Wealth of Nations*, and some to Ricardo and Marx. Thus, we let these three be the main representatives of different traditions in classical political economy, while other members only play a complementary role, in order to save space.

Adam Smith

Smith is sometimes called the father of economics. It is a moot point whether this is appropriate. The critics argue that the essentials of Smith's thought can be found in earlier authors. Even if this is the case, one cannot deny the magnificent role that his *Wealth of Nations* (1776) played in its systematic presentation of the relationships within the economy.

Smith was born in 1723 at Kirkcaldy in Scotland, and enrolled at the University of Glasgow at the age of fourteen. Here he came under the influence of the philosopher Francis Hutcheson, who lectured on economic issues and who brought Smith into contact with the philosopher David Hume. All three of them came to be leading figures in the Scottish Enlightenment.

Having, among other things, spent six years at Oxford – then a decadent university, however with excellent libraries – Smith was appointed professor of logic at Glasgow in 1751. He soon changed the chair of logic for that of moral philosophy. In 1759 he published his first major work, *The Theory of Moral Sentiments*. Smith left university in 1764 in order to accompany the Duke of Buccleuch as a tutor on a study tour to France. During the latter part of his stay in France, Smith took part in the meetings of the physiocrats. The foreign tour lasted two years, and during this time Smith began to write his *Wealth of Nations*. This grand work required several years of toil after his return, before it could be published in 1776. Two years later Smith accepted the post of Commissioner of Customs in Scotland, a post he handled with such zeal that after seven years he was able to report that the revenues were at least four times as large as when he took office.

Like other learned men of his time, Smith published within several fields: moral philosophy, the history of astronomy, the origin of language, the relationship between music, dance and poetry, etc. Yet his economic writings were clearly most influential, and we shall now focus on the ideas he presented in the *Wealth of Nations*. All the following quotations are taken from that book.

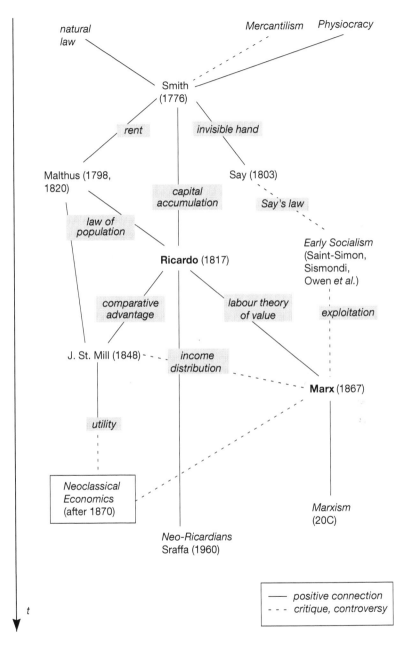

Figure 2 Classical political economy

Human characteristics

The characteristics of human beings are fundamental for Smith's view of how the economy works. Inherited character can, according to Smith, be modified to some extent by education, but must in the main be accepted as it is. The institutions of society should be based on this presumption. Which characteristics did Smith find in human beings? First, man is selfish and tries to better his position. These characteristics can actually cause society to progress, even when the conditions are not ideal. In his critique of Quesnay, Smith wrote:

> He seems not to have considered that, in the political body, the natural effort which every man is continually making to better his own condition is a principle of preservation capable of preventing and correcting, in many respects, the bad effects of a political economy, in some degree, both partial and oppressive. Such a political economy, though it no doubt retards more or less, is not always capable of stopping altogether the natural progress of a nation towards wealth and prosperity, and still less of making it go backwards.
>
> (p. 674)

Smith was, however, aware that there are exceptions to the rule that man strives to better his situation. He discussed drunkenness and gluttony, and condemned prodigality as a result of 'the passion for present enjoyment' (p. 341). The 'capricious man of fashion' was also considered deplorable, but fortunately 'this folly could, from the nature of things, extend to so few, that it could make no sensible impression upon the general employment of the people' (p. 469).

Does Smith's normal man have any further characteristics other than self-interest? A related characteristic is his 'propensity to truck, barter, and exchange one thing for another' (p. 25). This characteristic is unique to man. 'Nobody ever saw a dog make a fair and deliberate exchange of one bone for another with another dog' (p. 26). In addition to man's inclinations, there is another essential fact: different individuals are quite similar to begin with. 'The difference between the most dissimilar characters, between a philosopher and a common street porter, for example, seems to arise not so much from nature, as from habit, custom, and education' (pp. 28–9). However, the inclination to bargain and exchange results in a specialization that reinforces the original differences between people.

Division of labour – good and bad

The inclination to bargain and exchange is the ultimate cause of the division of labour, which has resulted in a considerable increase in production due to specialization. At the beginning of the *Wealth of Nations*, the division of labour is described in the positive terms of a great rise in productivity:

> It is the great multiplication of the productions of all the different arts, in consequence of the division of labour, which occasions, in a well-governed society, that universal opulence which extends itself to the lowest ranks of the people.
>
> (p. 22)

At the end of the *Wealth of Nations*, a more gloomy picture of the division of labour is given.

> In the progress of the division of labour, the employment of the far greater part of those who live by labour, that is, of the great body of the people, comes to be confined to a few very simple operations, frequently to one or two. But the understandings of the greater part of men are necessarily formed by their ordinary employments.
>
> (pp. 781–7)

Therefore, a man whose work is restricted to a few simple operations 'becomes as stupid and ignorant as it is possible for a human creature to become' (p. 782). The division of labour will impair not only his mental capability:

> It corrupts even the activity of his body, and renders him incapable of exerting his strength with vigour and perseverance in any other employment than that to which he has been bred. His dexterity at his own particular trade seems, in this manner, to be acquired at the expense of his intellectual, social, and martial virtues. But in every improved and civilised society this is the state into which the labouring poor, that is, the great body of the people, must necessarily fall, unless government takes some pains to prevent it.
>
> (p. 782)

While the division of labour greatly improves the material living conditions of all people – and, in fact, all nations by way of foreign trade – it impairs the workers' mental and physical condition. The dual character of the division of labour has consequences for Smith's view of liberty and the role of the state.

Natural liberty and the invisible hand

Adam Smith was well acquainted with the thoughts of the philosophers of natural law, such as Hugo Grotius and Samuel von Pufendorf (see Chapter 2). Smith's use of the term *natural liberty* and similar expressions is an indication of this influence. Examining the contexts in which Smith used the notion of natural liberty, we get an idea of the rather complex understanding that he had of it. Thus, we find that it meant freedom to change profession, and freedom to live in the parish where one has chosen to reside. It meant freedom both in domestic and international trade.

We encounter other examples where Smith held that natural liberty should *not* prevail even though it was, in express terms, *natural*. To restrain people from taking a great financial risk by accepting unbacked promissory notes from a banker, or to restrain a banker from issuing such notes is a manifest violation of natural liberty. The same applies to the obligation to build firewalls or to follow other safety regulations. However, 'exertions of the natural liberty of a few individuals, which might endanger the security of the whole society, are, and ought to be, restrained by the laws of all governments' (p. 324). Thus we see that Smith was no dogmatic advocate of unlimited liberties. He was guided by pragmatic considerations. If natural liberty could inflict damage upon society, it should be restricted. In all other cases the basic rule of liberty should apply. The human characteristics – self-interest and the inclination to trade – would then foster the common best, even though individuals would act in a self-seeking fashion.

> It is not from the benevolence of the butcher, the brewer, or the baker, that we expect our dinner, but from their regard to their own interest. We address ourselves, not to their humanity but to their self-love, and never talk to them of our own necessities but of their advantages.
>
> (pp. 26–7)

In this connection we may mention the *invisible hand*. None of Smith's expressions is as well-known as this one, although he himself used it only in passing. In the *Wealth of Nations*, it appears just once:

> As every individual . . . endeavours as much as he can both to employ his capital in the support of domestic industry, and so to direct that industry that its produce may be of the greatest value; every individual necessarily labours to render the annual revenue of the society as great as he can. He generally, indeed, neither intends to promote the public interest, nor knows how much he is promoting it. By preferring the support of domestic to that of foreign industry, he intends only his own security; and by directing that industry in such a manner as its produce

may be of the greatest value, he intends only his own gain, and he is in this, as in many other cases, led by an invisible hand to promote an end which was no part of his intention.

(p. 456)

According to Smith's principal rule, the allocation of resources would be most efficient if each capitalist were able to invest his capital according to his own preferences, and every person could choose her occupation and pursue her business without legal obstacles. The invisible hand is a metaphor for the conditions that produce this correspondence between self-interest and the best for society. The idea was not new. It could be found, for instance, in the writings of the Greek Church Father John Chrysostom (349–c. 407) who regarded the connection between self-interest and common interest as part of a divine plan. Yet the idea was rarely formulated as clearly as by Adam Smith.

However, Smith's principal rule was merely a principle, and he himself demonstrated that natural liberty does not always yield the best result, neither in a narrow economic sense nor in a wider human sense. We have already seen that, in Smith's opinion, natural liberty should be restricted when it would harm society as a whole. We have also seen that the division of labour that emerges spontaneously in a free society tends to impair the mental and physical fitness of the workers. Nor is free trade always advantageous to all parties. As Smith wrote with reference to transatlantic trade and the discovery and conquest of the Americas, 'the savage injustice of the Europeans rendered an event, which ought to have been beneficial to all, ruinous and destructive to several of those unfortunate countries' (p. 448).

What the government should and should not do

In Smith's opinion, the government should interfere less in economic life than it did in Britain, where mercantilists ruled the roost. Smith had three arguments against this. First, he was critical of mercantilism as a doctrine and political practice. Regulation of trade and production had been carried out after lobbying by merchants and manufacturers, and it had led to an inefficient allocation of resources. The privileges of the guilds and the licensed monopolies favoured a few at the expense of the majority of the people. Smith repeatedly made statements like: 'That it was the spirit of monopoly which both invented and propagated this doctrine cannot be doubted; and they who first taught it were by no means such fools as they who believed it' (p. 493).

A second argument is related to the inability of the government to regulate the economy in the interest of the majority of the people:

The statesman who should attempt to direct private people in what manner they ought to employ their capitals would not only load himself with a most unnecessary attention, but assume an authority which could safely be trusted, not only to no single person, but to no council or senate whatever.

(p. 456)

Smith's third argument against a large public sector is more implicit in his distinction between productive and unproductive labour. Productive labour is manifested in a good that remains when the production process is completed. Manufacturing and agricultural work are good examples. Unproductive labour includes different kinds of services. Such labour perishes in the same moment as it has been performed. Here Smith includes the sovereign, together with all civil and military servants, churchmen, lawyers, physicians, buffoons, musicians, opera-singers, etc. They are maintained by the produce of the productive labourers, 'how honourable, how useful, or how necessary soever' their services are (p. 331). (Compare this with the more restrictive view of the physiocrats according to which all sectors except agriculture are sterile.) If the unproductive became too numerous, their maintenance would require so large a part of the produce that it would be necessary to draw on capital. The produce would gradually diminish. Smith argued that 'great nations are never impoverished by private, though they sometimes are by publick prodigality and misconduct. The whole, or almost the whole publick revenue, is in most countries employed in maintaining unproductive hands' (p. 342).

Smith did not, however, want to preclude government commitments. The government has three main duties, and Smith mentioned a number of other involvements with approval, too. The first main duty is to protect the society from invasion, i.e. to maintain a national defence. The second duty is to protect each member of the society from injustice or oppression by other members, i.e. to establish an administration of justice. These two duties of protection are the minimum activity required by any state. However, with the third duty Smith went beyond that minimum. The third duty is

that of erecting and maintaining those publick institutions and those publick works, which, though they may be in the highest degree advantageous to a great society, are, however, of such a nature, that the profit could never repay the expence to any individual or small number of individuals, and which it, therefore, cannot be expected that any individual or small number of individuals should erect or maintain.

(p. 723)

Smith was aware of what modern analysis calls collective goods and external effects. He discussed such things as roads, bridges, canals, harbours, postal services, and in particular institutions for education that would help to counteract the detrimental effects of the division of labour on the workers. The fact that the government has to guarantee that they will be established does not mean that they should be completely financed by taxes. Fees paid by users may also sometimes be appropriate, according to Smith.

In addition to the three main duties of government, there are examples of other forms of intervention that Smith supported. They show that he was a pragmatic, rather than dogmatic, advocate of *laissez faire*. Fundamentally, Smith advocated free trade between nations, but he argued cases in which it is appropriate to favour domestic interests by the aid of customs and other regulations. The first such case is activities necessary for the defence of the country. Thus he described the Navigation Act, which restricted foreign shipping in the trade of England – by later economists interpreted as one of the strongest acts of protectionism in history – as 'perhaps the wisest of all the commercial regulations of England' (p. 465). It guaranteed the existence of British sailors and shipping, which was important for the naval defence. Another case is when a tax is imposed on a domestic industry. An equivalent customs duty would then leave the competition between domestic and imported goods on the same footing as before the tax was introduced.

Value

In the theory of value, Smith and other classical economists introduced a distinction that dates back to Aristotle, but has been abandoned by modern price theory. It is the distinction between value in use and value in exchange. Smith argued:

> The word value, it is to be observed, has two different meanings, and sometimes expresses the utility of some particular object, and sometimes the power of purchasing other goods which the possession of that object conveys. The one may be called 'value in use'; the other, 'value in exchange'. The things which have the greatest value in use have frequently little or no value in exchange; and, on the contrary, those which have the greatest value in exchange have frequently little or no value in use. Nothing is more useful than water: but it will purchase scarce anything; scarce anything can be had in exchange for it. A diamond, on the contrary, has scarce any value in use; but a very great quantity of other goods may frequently be had in exchange for it.
>
> (pp. 44–5)

The last problem in the quotation – why useful things like water can be so cheap while useless things like diamonds are so expensive – is known as the paradox of value. Smith was not the first person to discuss it. It was explained fairly adequately in Plato's *Euthydemus* – 'only what is rare is valuable', reappeared in Pufendorf, and was completely dissolved by the neoclassical analysis of marginal utility in the 1870s. Smith devoted much effort to explaining the value in exchange, i.e. the price. We can discern at least three different theories. First, he had a crude *labour theory of value*:

> If among a nation of hunters, for example, it usually costs twice the labour to kill a beaver which it does to kill a deer, one beaver should naturally exchange for or be worth two deer. It is natural that what is usually the produce of two days or two hours' labour, should be worth double of what is usually the produce of one day's or one hour's labour.
>
> (p. 65)

Next, a modification is introduced: If some kind of labour is unusually severe or requires an uncommon degree of dexterity or ingenuity, this will give a higher value to its produce than what would be due to the amount of working time. The crude labour theory of value – the idea that the relative prices of goods reflect the ratio of labour inputs in their production – was deemed to hold for 'that early and rude state of society which precedes both the accumulation of stock and the appropriation of land' (p. 63). In more developed societies – where machines and other kinds of capital are used in production and where land is privately owned – price formation is more complicated. Here, Smith took recourse to a more general theory of prices based on costs of production. Not all of the product will go to labour; part of it will accrue to the owner of the capital used in the process. A third part will be taken by the landlord: 'As soon as the land of any country has all become private property, the landlords, like all other men, love to reap where they never sowed, and demand a rent even for its natural produce' (p. 67). The worker, the capitalist and the landlord were different persons in Smith's world. Wages, profit and rent form the price of each good: '[I]n every improved society, all the three enter more or less, as component parts, into the price of the far greater part of commodities' (p. 68).

Smith had a third complementary theory in which prices are determined by demand and supply. The basic assumption is that there is a *natural* price that prevails when wages, rent and profit are at their 'ordinary' level. The prices of all commodities continually gravitate towards their natural price. However, occasional variations in demand and supply may cause the market price to deviate temporarily from the natural price. In this way, the consumer or the demand side also appears in Smith's price theory. The production side is, however, the most important. With the first neoclassical authors in the 1870s, the emphasis came to be reversed (see Chapter 5).

Distribution of income

Smith is sometimes criticized for not giving a clear explanation of how the levels of wages, profits and rents are determined, and how the result of the production is divided between these three kinds of income. This does not mean that attempts at explanation are absent in his work. The level of wages is considered to be a result mainly of the prosperity of the society and the amount of capital. It also depends on the agreeableness of the profession, the efforts required to learn it, the trust people must have in those who practise the profession, and the certainty of gaining a livelihood from the profession. The profit increases with the risk, decreases with the agreeableness of the industry and decreases in relative terms if the capital grows. Here, we find an indication of a theory of decreasing returns which will play an important role later on. The rent, i.e. the price for leasing land, is considered both as a monopoly price determined by the landlord and as a residual that remains after wages and profit have been deducted from the price.

Jean-Baptiste Say

The Frenchman Say read Smith's *Wealth of Nations* when he was about twenty, and fifteen years later he published his *Traité d'économie politique* (1803), a treatise on political economy that came out in five different editions during Say's lifetime. This work was instrumental in the dissemination of Smith's ideas on the European continent, and, in an English translation, even in the USA.

At least two things may be said about Say. First, he has sometimes been regarded as a pioneer of the subjective theory of value that later on came into full bloom with the neoclassical economists. Price measures value, and value measures utility, according to Say. Consequently, utility is the foundation of price. In emphasizing the subjective utility that individuals experience, Say differs from most other classical authors, especially Ricardo, who accentuated the labour spent in production as the factor creating value.

Second, Say is mostly remembered for *Say's law* which holds that, as soon as a good has been produced, it offers a market for other goods corresponding to its whole value. The underlying argument is that all production provides income for the production factors that will be spent in the markets. As a simple slogan, Say's law is often formulated as 'supply creates its own demand'. This expression must not be interpreted to mean that the supply of a certain good creates an equal demand for the same good. An excess supply of some types of goods may arise, but it would be balanced by excess demand for other goods, such that total demand in the economy could never fall short of supply. If it is to mean more than a mere identity of aggregate income and expenditure in the circular flow of goods, Say's law rejects the argument that economic crises can be explained as results of a lack in the aggregate demand for goods. There has been much scholarly debate about the interpretation of Say's law in its different versions, spelt out in the five editions of the *Traité* published between 1803 and 1806. The strongest objections to Say's law are based on the argument that the hoarding of money and contraction of credit at times when real and financial investors turn pessimistic can indeed lead to situations in which aggregate demand falls short of the aggregate supply of goods.

Thomas Robert Malthus

The Englishman Malthus had studied philosophy, mathematics and theology before taking holy orders in 1790. In 1805 he became professor of history and political economy at East India College near London. He is famous for his population studies, but he also made important contributions to other areas of political economy. The pessimistic theory of population that Malthus presented in his classical *Essay on the Principle of Population* (1798) was principally supported by Ricardo and John Stuart Mill, and later became the foundation of neo-Malthusianism. His main point is apparent in the following quotation:

I think I may fairly make two postulata.

First, That food is necessary to the existence of man.

Secondly, That the passion between the sexes is necessary and will remain nearly in its present state.

These two laws, ever since we have had any knowledge of mankind, appear to have been fixed laws of our nature, and as we have not hitherto seen any alteration in them, we have no right to conclude that they will ever cease to be what they now are . . .

Assuming then my postulata as granted, I say, that the power of population is indefinitely greater than the power in the earth to produce subsistence for men.

Population, when unchecked, increases in a geometrical ratio. Subsistence increases only in an arithmetical ratio. A slight acquaintance with numbers will shew the immensity of the first power in comparison of the second.

By that law of our nature which makes food necessary to the life of man, the effects of these two unequal powers must be kept equal.

This implies a strong and constantly operating check on population from the difficulty of subsistence. This difficulty must fall somewhere and must necessarily be severely felt by a large portion of mankind.

(pp. 70–1)

What will be the consequence? Misery and vice. The wage rate will be forced down to the subsistence level, an idea that later on is found also in the work of his friend David Ricardo. Malthus revised his essay in several editions. There is a substantial difference between the first edition and the second (1803), in which he introduces, for example, postponed marriages among those factors that can bring the growth of population into line with the growth of subsistence.

More than twenty years after the population essay, Malthus published his *Principles of Political Economy* (1820). The book belongs to the classical tradition, but is regarded as an unorthodox work. In price theory, Malthus elaborated the concepts of supply and demand further, rejecting Say's law and the idea that the economy spontaneously gives full employment. He presented elements of underconsumption and oversaving theories. While Say considered economic development as being determined by aggregate supply only, Malthus pointed out that it could be restricted by a lack of demand. There is a link between this idea and those of Keynes some hundred years later (see Chapter 6).

David Ricardo

David Ricardo was born into a wealthy family in London in 1772. His parents were immigrants from Amsterdam. His father was a stockbroker, and at the age of fourteen David began working with him. Seven years later he broke with his parents as he left Judaism and married a Quaker. His own energy and help from his friends at the Exchange made it nevertheless possible for him to continue as a successful stockbroker, and he soon became wealthy. In the 1810s he was an influential participant in discussions on monetary policy, where he explained the English inflation with an excessive issue of bank-notes. He also took a position in favour of free trade, and criticized the restrictions on the importing of corn. In 1819 he bought a seat of an Irish constituency and he became a member of Parliament.

David Ricardo was perhaps less pioneering than Smith, on whose ideas he largely based his theory. His reputation as an economist is nevertheless at least as good as Smith's, because of the acumen that characterizes his analysis. Ricardo's most important work is *On the Principles of Political Economy, and Taxation* (1817). Essential parts of the book are devoted to the functional distribution of income, i.e. the distribution between workers, capitalists and landlords. The theory of value is an important related element. Ricardo's theory of the rent of land has marginalistic elements which heralds neoclassical thought (see Chapter 5). The chapter on machinery in the third edition of his *Principles* (1821) is an early analysis of the employment effects of technical progress, where Ricardo held that investment in new machinery may, under certain conditions, increase long-term unemployment. Ricardo's most celebrated contribution is probably his theory of comparative advantages in international trade. Yet his greatest legacy to modern economics is perhaps his method of reasoning. He worked with theoretical models and developed the deductive method within economics, usually starting with a number of assumptions, from which he deduced his theorems in clear logical steps. This compares to the more inductive reasoning of Smith, who often started from observations of the real world in order to discuss the principles and to draw general conclusions. The rigorous re-examination of Smith's insights with his deductive method lets Ricardo stand out as the second great protagonist of the classical school. In the following, we expand a little on some of his observations on the principles of political economy.

On value

Ricardo's first chapter in the *Principles* is on value, which demonstrates the fundamental importance this question had to him. Adam Smith's distinction between value in use and value in exchange was his starting point. Like Smith he mostly used *value* as synonymous with *value in exchange* or *exchangeable value*.

Ricardo refined Smith's labour theory of value. He explicitly changed the assumptions over and over again and deduced his conclusions in case after case. To have exchangeable value, a commodity must possess utility. Possessing utility, the commodity derives exchangeable value from two sources: from its scarcity and from the quantity of labour required to obtain it. For some commodities, like rare statues, pictures, books or coins, their scarcity is the only source of exchange value. As their quantity cannot be increased, their value is independent of the quantity of labour used in their production. Such commodities form, however, only a minor part of the commodities exchanged in the market. Therefore, Ricardo leaves them aside and focuses on 'such commodities only as can be increased in quantity by the exertion of human industry, and on the production of which competition operates without restraint' (p. 12).

Adam Smith's statement that, if it usually costs twice the labour to kill a beaver which it costs to kill a deer, one beaver should naturally exchange for two deer, is also Ricardo's point of departure. Like Smith, he is aware that this principle needs qualification in less simple cases. Labour may be of different qualities, but when the market has taken account of this the wage differentials tend to be quite stable over time, and so will the relative value of commodities. Labour may be used not only immediately in the production of consumption goods but also indirectly, i.e. in the production of intermediate goods. Such indirect labour will also be included in the value of the consumption good:

If we suppose the occupations of the society extended, that some provide canoes and tackle necessary for fishing, others the seed and rude machinery first used in agriculture, still the same principle would hold true, that the exchangeable value of the commodities produced would be in proportion to the labour bestowed on their production; not on the immediate production only, but on all those implements or machines required to give effect to the particular labour to which they were applied.

(p. 24)

The principle that the relation between the quantities of immediate labour in the production of different commodities regulates the relative value of the commodities has to be modified when the proportions of indirect to immediate labour differ. Intermediate goods, such as machines, are of different durability and may require different quantities of labour when they are produced. 'The proportions, too, in which the capital that is to support labour, and the capital that is invested in tools, machinery, and buildings, may be variously combined' (p. 30). Ricardo hinted at a complication that later came to play an important role in Marx's struggle with the theory of value. When, in the production of various goods, the relative inputs of immediate labour and indirect labour (real capital) differ, the relative market prices of those goods will diverge from the relation between the total labour inputs in their production. The reason behind this is the tendency towards a uniform rate of profit, established by way of competition between the capitalists. When Ricardo left the most simplifying assumptions, he gradually receded from the labour theory of value, which was reduced to a rough approximation.

The real capital that is to support labour, for instance food and clothing, is called *circulating capital*. Durable implements like machinery and buildings are *fixed capital*. Ricardo took this distinction over from Smith and used, like Smith (and many others), the word capital in more than one sense. Sometimes it denotes real capital, i.e. physical capital goods, such as 'machinery and other fixed and durable capital' (p. 30). In other cases it means an amount of money, as in the expression 'a shoemaker, whose capital is chiefly employed in the payment of wages, which are expended on food and clothing' (p. 31).

On rent

Ricardo's theory of the rent of land is historically interesting because it is an early elaborate example of the marginal principle and diminishing returns, which later on became central in neoclassical thought. There is one difference, however. While neoclassical analysis mainly deals with the result of a marginal change of an input factor of constant quality, Ricardo set the focus on inputs, especially land, of different quality. According to his definition, '[r]ent is that portion of the produce of the earth, which is paid to the landlord for the use of the original and indestructible powers of the soil' (p. 67). If there were an abundance of fertile land at an excellent location, only a small portion of it would be cultivated. Land would be a free good; no rent would be paid. However, when population grows, land of inferior quality will have to be cultivated, and rent will be paid for the better land.

Let us take a look at Ricardo's basic example. Suppose there are three plots of land: Nos 1, 2 and 3, each of equal size, but different quality. With an equal amount of capital and labour on each plot, a net produce of 100, 90 and 80 quarters of corn could be harvested on each respective plot (see Table 2).

> In a new country, where there is an abundance of fertile land compared with the population, and where therefore it is only necessary to cultivate No. 1, the whole net produce will belong to the cultivator, and will be the profits of the stock which he advances. As soon as population had so far increased as to make it necessary to cultivate No. 2, from which ninety quarters only can be obtained after supporting the labourers, rent would commence on No. 1; for either there must be two rates of profit on agricultural capital, or ten quarters . . . must be withdrawn from the produce of No. 1, for some other purpose.
>
> (pp. 70–1)

That other purpose is rent. If the population were to grow further, No. 3 would also be cultivated, the rent on No. 1 would increase, and there would be rent on No. 2, too, which would result in the following situation.

The driving force that generates rent is, again, the tendency towards profit equalization inherent in the competition between capitalists. Since even the marginal plot of land must yield some profit in order to be cultivated, the market price (value in exchange) will attain a level at which more fertile plots, where unit costs are lower, yield extra profits. As the capitalists compete for the lease or ownership of the more fertile plots, the extra profits are transformed into payments of rent to the landlords.

The same principle can be applied to other natural resources of 'various qualities' (p. 75). If they can be appropriated, and if the access to each quality is limited, they afford a rent, as the successive qualities are brought into use. Beyond natural resources Ricardian rent theory can be extended to explain, for example, price differences between identical types of buildings (private housing, offices, shops, etc.) in different locations. At the end of the chapter, Ricardo illustrated how a similar result may be obtained if, instead, different portions of capital were employed on a certain piece of land.

For Ricardo, it was not sufficient to establish the fundamental principles in an unalterable world. The industrial revolution had started and he saw the

Table 2 Ricardo's rent example

Quality of land	Produce	Rent
No. 1	100	20
No. 2	90	10
No. 3	80	0
Total	270	30

changes around him. The question of growth was important, and the effects of population growth and technical progress (improved machinery, rotation of crops, etc.) were analysed. This did not exclude a belief that the net effects of such developments and of diminishing returns to land would in the long run lead to a stationary state, i.e. to an economy without growth.

On foreign trade

Ricardo regarded free international trade as highly beneficial for a country. In one of the few poetic paragraphs of his *Principles* he describes the relation between the striving for individual advantage and the wealth of the nation in terms that are reminiscent of Smith's invisible hand:

> Under a system of perfectly free commerce, each country naturally devotes its capital and labour to such employments as are most beneficial to each. This pursuit of individual advantage is admirably connected with the universal good of the whole. By stimulating industry, by regarding ingenuity, and by using most efficaciously the peculiar powers bestowed by nature, it distributes labour most effectively and most economically: while by increasing the general mass of productions, it diffuses general benefit, and binds together by one common tie of interest and inter-course, the universal society of nations throughout the civilized world. It is this principle which determines that wine shall be made in France and Portugal, that corn shall be grown in America and Poland, and that hardware and other goods shall be manufactured in England.
>
> (pp. 133–4)

The most famous part in Ricardo's chapter on foreign trade is his analysis of comparative advantages (or comparative costs), which shows that it is practically always feasible to specialize and trade with each other. His concrete example is still found in modern textbooks. To begin with, it is assumed that both Portugal and England would be able to produce their wine and cloth. In Portugal the production of wine might require the labour of

80 persons for one year, i.e. 80 personyears, and cloth the labour of 90 persons. In England the production of the same quantity of wine and cloth might require 120 and 100 personyears, respectively, i.e.

	Cloth	Wine
England	100	120
Portugal	90	80

Portuguese producers are thus more efficient than English producers in both branches. If labour and capital would move freely between countries, it 'would undoubtedly be advantageous to the capitalists of England, and to the consumers in both countries, that under such circumstances the wine and cloth should both be made in Portugal, and therefore that the capital and labour of England employed in making cloth, should be removed to Portugal for that purpose' (p. 136). But labour and capital do not move freely between countries. Concerning labour, Ricardo seems to have regarded its immobility as self-evident. With regard to capital he, like Smith in his paragraph on the invisible hand, invoked a *home bias* argument: for the capitalist it is safer and easier to invest his money in the domestic economy, even if it yields a lower rate of profit there than abroad (pp. 136–7).

Given the limited mobility of production factors, it is advantageous to England to export cloth to and import wine from Portugal, and this trade will even benefit Portugal. So the 'exchange might even take place, notwithstanding that the commodity imported by Portugal could be produced there with less labour than in England' (p. 135). In comparison with Portugal, England is *comparatively* more efficient in producing cloth than wine, as 100/90, the relative cost of producing cloth, is less than 120/80, the relative cost of producing wine. Portugal is *comparatively* more efficient in producing wine, as 80/120 is less than 90/100. This leads to the conclusion that total production could be increased by specialization and trade. If 90 + 80 Portuguese produce only wine and 100 + 120 Englishmen produce only cloth, the production of both wine and cloth is increased. By making use of their comparative advantage in production, all countries can make gains from foreign trade.

John Stuart Mill

With John Stuart Mill classical political economy reached its peak of contemporary influence. Mill was basically a philosopher, brought up in the spirit of scientific thinking by his father James Mill. He contributed to logic and became a prominent spokesman of utilitarianism, a theory in moral philosophy according to which human actions should be governed and judged by the public and private utility caused by the action. Mill's *On Liberty* (1859) has been very important for liberal views on the freedom of speech and the relation between the individual and the government. Mill's attitude of *laissez faire* was more pronounced towards freedom of expression than towards economic and social problems.

Mill's broad approach is suggested by the title of his main economic work *Principles of Political Economy, with some of their Applications to Social Philosophy* (1848), which became the bible of the economists in the second half of the nineteenth century. Mill argued that Ricardo had, in principle, solved all the essential problems of economic theory and that he himself was only extending and qualifying Ricardian doctrine. But the wide range of social issues that Mill addressed is more reminiscent of Smith, and he was both eclectic and innovative. He included new elements in his *Principles*, such as the concept of opportunity costs and a refined abstinence theory of interest, that were not fully consistent with the cornerstones of the Ricardian doctrine. Like most other classical economists, Mill foresaw a future when the economy has reached a stationary state, i.e. growth has come to an end. According to Mill, that state is not necessarily bad. It may imply that man, liberated from the idea of incessant material progress, may find the peace of mind for loftier purposes.

Karl Marx

In any science or art, the word *classical* can be understood as referring to a well-established, defining mode of thought and expression – a 'best practice' of the past that has set standards for the present. Classical political economy certainly has played that role for current economic thinking, but it is classical also in another sense that has come to be neglected in modern economics: it defined the key agents in the economy in terms of classes. Modifying the class concept of physiocracy (see Chapter 2), classical political economy distinguished between capitalists, labourers and landlords, based on the underlying factors of production (capital, labour and land) and the respective sources of income (profits, wages and rent). In the tradition of Smith and Ricardo, most classical writers considered the capitalists to be the driving force. By their investments and accumulation of capital, they would expand production and the market system until all opportunities to make additional profits are exhausted. The (more or less) happy end of the story was thus a stationary state in which the economy continues reproducing itself without growth, and with a constant distribution of income between the classes. This rather harmonious vision was challenged by Karl Marx and his followers who used Ricardian theory to argue that 'the capitalist mode of production' is based on an unsustainable exploitation of the labourers. Class struggle would sooner or later lead to a revolution that transforms the system into socialism.

Marx was born in 1818 at Trier, then part of the Rhineland province of Prussia. After studies in law, philosophy and history at Bonn and Berlin, and a doctorate in philosophy at Jena, Marx became a journalist and editor of the *Rheinische Zeitung*, a liberal newspaper. In the years preceding 1848, when uprisings and democratic revolutions took place in several European countries, Marx was politically very active, turning increasingly radical and helping to found the Communist League in 1847. Together with Friedrich Engels (1820–95), his lifelong friend and sponsor, he published the *Communist Manifesto* (1848) as the programme of the League. The idea that capitalism is a transitory stage in a history full of class struggles was already present in the *Manifesto*.

After various stages of prosecution and exile in Paris, Brussels and elsewhere, Marx settled in London in 1849, where he came to stay for the rest of his life. He attempted to give his political views a scientific base by a critical examination and extension of the economic writings of his time. Like the early socialists – such as Claude Henri de Rouvrouy Saint-Simon (1760–1825), Robert Owen (1771–1858) and Léonard Simonde de Sismondi (1773–1842) – Marx opposed private ownership of the means of production. In his view, however, the early socialists were unable to provide a proper explanation of the 'laws of motion' of capitalism. Marx was much more fascinated by Ricardo's method of deducing specific conclusions from general assumptions, and he linked up Ricardo's method with the philosopher Hegel's dialectics, which he had studied extensively during his formative years. After nearly two decades of studying classical political economy and other literature, Marx published volume I of his major work *Das Kapital* – in English: *Capital: A Critique of Political Economy* – in 1867. Volumes II and III were published posthumously, in 1885 and 1894. In the following, we outline some of the main ideas contained in the three volumes.

On value and capital

In Marx's view the main characteristic of the contemporary mode of production was the production and accumulation of capital through the *exploitation* of labourers in a market system based on *equal* exchange. This may, at first, look paradoxical, but followed from a specific combination of classical arguments. Like Smith and Ricardo, Marx opened his analysis with a discussion of the concepts of value. In a capitalist society, commodities are produced mainly for the market, and each commodity has two sides: the natural form or use value, and the social form of being exchangeable. According to Marx, the exchange value is the manifest form of the human labour materialized in the commodity. Marx applied the same logic to money, the general equivalent in exchange. In his time, money was still backed by metallic reserves (gold and silver) and hence, too, a product of labour, the only 'value-creating substance'. However, not all labour forms value. There is the important qualification of *socially necessary* labour in the sense that it is only the average input that counts.

> The total labour-power of society, which is manifested in the values of the world of commodities, counts here as one homogenous mass of human labour-power, although composed of innumerable individual units of labour-power. Each of these units . . . only needs, in order to produce a commodity, the labour time which is necessary on an average, or in other words, . . . the labour-time required to produce any use-value under the conditions of production normal for a given society and with the average degree of skill and intensity of labour prevalent in that society.
>
> (*Capital*, vol. I, p. 129)

In order to find an analytical base for his exploitation argument, Marx thus returned to the labour theory of value from which Ricardo, in his *Principles*, had receded with increasing sophistication. Marx defined 'labour-power' as a commodity that workers, who normally have no other source of income, put at the disposal of their employers by selling it for a certain period. In competition the average wage tends to coincide with the value of labour-power, which is determined by the labour input necessary to reproduce the labour-power by way of feeding, sheltering and educating the working person. However, Marx argued that labour-power is a specific commodity which can create a value that is larger than its cost of reproduction. It is a commodity that can generate a surplus value in excess of its price, i.e. the wage rate paid in the labour market.

This is where capital comes into the picture. According to Marx's definition of the capitalist mode of production, commodities are essentially produced in order to transform an invested sum of money into a greater sum, yielding a profit. Capitalists buy means of production (machinery, raw materials, etc.) and labour-power, and combine them to produce the commodities that they then sell. Given a large supply of labour (which Marx explains as an endogenous outcome of capitalism – see below), the average working time is longer than that required to cover the costs of reproduction of both labour and capital. The surplus is appropriated by the capitalists as they pay wages in equal exchange of money for the services of labour. It is the source of profits, i.e. the rate of return to the invested capital. Profits are, at least in part, re-invested in the expansion of the capital stock and the hiring of more labour.

Hence, capital accumulation is, in Marx's view, based on the exploitation of labour.

On reproduction, growth and crises

In volumes II and III of *Capital*, the focus was set on the production, circulation and reproduction of 'social aggregate capital'. Building on Quesnay's analysis of the circular flow of goods and money (see Chapter 2), Marx discussed the conditions at which a capitalist economy would keep evolving over time. With his famous 'schemes of reproduction' (vol. II, part three) he provided a macroeconomic model in which the economy was divided into two sectors. Sector I produces means of production, in modern language: capital goods, while sector II produces consumer goods. At the first stage, Marx examined the sectoral and sequential requirements of *simple reproduction*, i.e. the proportionality and timing of the production and circulation of different goods required for keeping the economy in a stationary state. At the second stage, he proceeded to the analysis of *extended reproduction*, i.e. the conditions of a growing economy. Marx's pattern of analysis influenced the twentieth century literature on business cycles and growth, even though he is rarely cited.

Marx held the view, expounded in volume III, that the growth process of capitalist economies is cyclical, i.e. accompanied by crises, and that it will eventually end in revolution and transformation to a socialist system. The underlying argument was related to structural change in the composition of aggregate capital. Modifying the classical terminology of fixed and circulating capital, Marx considered total capital, K, as being divided in 'constant', c, and 'variable capital', v, such that $K = c + v$. The total sum of wage payments was considered as variable capital, since the outlay on value-creating labour leads to an increase of capital by way of generating surplus value, s. 'Constant capital' accordingly denotes the outlay on all other inputs (machinery, buildings, etc.) whose value is transferred onto the output, but not augmented as such.

In a simplified form the profit rate, r, could thus be defined as: $r = s/K = s/(c+v)$. In the course of economic development, capital accumulation would finance the increased use of machinery and other constant capital, in order to enhance the productivity of labour and hence raise total profits. According to Marx, however, the corresponding rise in capital intensity, c/v, would have two critical effects, leading to cyclical fluctuations and finally to the breakdown of the system. In the short run, productivity growth could be so strong that there would be periodical overproduction, or under-consumption, as workers' wages and other money incomes would not suffice to make demands equal to the supplies of commodities. Crises would develop, producing unemployment and further reductions in demand. The periodical crises would blow over with the fall in commodity prices and depreciation of constant capital, but they would leave their traces in the labour market. Due to the labour-saving effects of technical progress, each crisis would add further workers to a growing 'industrial reserve army' that depresses real wages by way of competition.

According to Marx, the long-run effect of the increase in capital intensity is a 'progressive tendency of the rate of profit to fall'; he even called it a 'law' (vol. III, ch. 13). As the share of constant capital grows, $r = s/K$ must decline, because surplus is created only by the diminishing share of variable capital. Marx listed a number of 'counteracting factors' that could slow down the fall of the average profit rate (vol. III, ch. 14), such as a cheapening of elements of constant capital, more intense exploitation of labour, or foreign trade. But he nevertheless predicted that the capitalist mode of production would break down due to its 'inner contradictions'. The decline in the profit rate and the growing immiserization of workers and the middle class in the wake of the cyclical crises would, sooner or later, lead to stagnation of investment, militant class struggle and finally the socialist revolution. It is well known that, in the course of the twentieth century, various communist and other parties acted as if Marx's prediction had come true. A number of Marxist writers, notably Rosa Luxemburg (1870–1919) and Rudolf Hilferding (1877–1941), attempted to update and extend Marx's macroeconomic theory. Some hundred years later, however, it seems that either Marx's construction of the 'law of the tendency of the profit rate to fall' is wrong or that the 'counteracting factors' are too strong.

What remains of classical economic thought?

Classical political economy is nowadays revered as the mother of modern neoclassical economics – in principle. In practice, it is mostly reduced to a stock of canonical citations, preferably from Smith or Mill. By modern standards, Smith's inductive method and anecdotal style, Ricardo's numerical examples, and Mill's and Marx's mixtures of positive and normative arguments are mostly considered as outdated modes of reflection. Even the label *political economy* used to be out of fashion, retained only by Marxian economists. In recent decades, the label has returned to the mainstream, but now denotes only the subfield where political behaviour is analysed by the methods of economics.

Yet it is hard to deny that some classical tenets and methods have survived in modern economics, of which a large part carries, after all, the label *neoclassical*. Ricardo's deductive method is still in use, and Smith's metaphor of the invisible hand can be used to characterize the core of neoclassical general equilibrium theory. Another prominent example is Ricardo's theory of comparative advantages. It has been further developed along neoclassical lines, with key contributions by Eli Heckscher (1879–1952), Bertil Ohlin (1899–79), Gottfried Haberler (1900–95), Wolfgang Stolper (1912–2002) and Paul Samuelson (1915–2009). One of the main innovations was to let the proportions of different factors of production determine the pattern of trade. Another was the replacement of direct costs of production by the concept of opportunity costs, which was already present in John Stuart Mill. Modern theories of international trade have further relaxed Ricardo's restrictive assumptions, introducing imperfect competition, factor mobility and other complications. Yet the basic conclusion of universal gains from specialization and trade has survived remarkably well.

The influences of Smith, Ricardo, Mill and Marx can also be identified in modern theories of business cycles, growth and development. A noteworthy, though not easily classifiable example is the theory of economic development by way of *creative destruction* that the Austrian Joseph Alois Schumpeter (1883–1950) developed from a combination of Smith's economic philosophy with Marx's theory of cyclical growth and other elements.

In the next chapter we will discuss neoclassical economics and its relation to classical political economy in greater detail. At this point, however, we should draw attention to the neo-Ricardian school that explicitly aims at reviving and reformulating classical ideas in opposition to neoclassical economics. The main protagonist of this school is the Italian Cambridge economist Piero Sraffa (1898–1983). In his *Production of Commodities by Means of Commodities* (1960) he showed that the system of prices of production can be determined without having to take recourse to the (neoclassical) principles of marginal productivity and marginal utility or to the (classical) labour theory of value, from which Ricardo had already gradually receded. The system of relative prices as well as the average profit rate (alternatively: the average wage rate) and rent can be derived from the data for the wage rate (alternatively: the profit rate), the level and structure of aggregate production, and the set of production techniques for the different commodities. If, for example, the wage rate rises, prices change and the profit rate falls. Prices and profits must thus be determined simultaneously. Demonstrating the dependence of relative prices on income distribution, the neo-Ricardian approach preserves a characteristic element of classical political economy.

References

Blaug, Mark (1997) *Economic Theory in Retrospect*, 5th ed. Cambridge: Cambridge University Press.

Kurz, Heinz D. and Salvadori, Neri (2000) Piero Sraffa's Contributions to Economics: A Brief Survey. In Kurz, Heinz D. (ed.), *Critical Essays on Piero Sraffa's Legacy in Economics*. Cambridge: Cambridge University Press.

Malthus, Thomas Robert (1798) [1970] *An Essay on the Principle of Population*. Harmondsworth: Penguin Books.

Marx, Karl (1867) [1976] *Capital: A Critique of Political Economy*, vol. I. Harmondsworth: Penguin Books.

Marx, Karl (1885) [1909] *Capital: A Critique of Political Economy*, vol. II: *The Process of Circulation of Capital*. Chicago, IL: Charles H. Kerr & Co.

Marx, Karl (1894) [1909] *Capital: A Critique of Political Economy*, vol. III: *The Process of Circulation of Capital*. Chicago, IL: Charles H. Kerr & Co.

Ricardo, David (1817, 1821 3rd ed.) [1951] *On the Principles of Political Economy, and Taxation* (The Works and Correspondence of David Ricardo, vol. I, ed. by Piero Sraffa). Cambridge: Cambridge University Press.

Ryan, Alan (1987) Mill, John Stuart. *The New Palgrave: A Dictionary of Economics*. London, Basingstoke: Macmillan.

Smith, Adam (1776) [1979] *An Inquiry into the Nature and Causes of the Wealth of Nations*. Ed. by R. H. Campbell, A. S. Skinner and W. B. Todd. Oxford: Clarendon Press.

Sowell, Thomas (1987) Say, Jean-Baptiste. *The New Palgrave: A Dictionary of Economics*. London, Basingstoke: Macmillan.

Spiegel, Henry William (1971) *The Growth of Economic Thought*. Durham, NC: Duke University Press.

4 Neoclassical economics

The neoclassical breakthrough is often dated to the 1870s. A characteristic feature of neoclassicism is its use of marginal concepts – such as marginal utility, marginal cost and marginal revenue – to determine the behaviour that drives the market forces of supply and demand. Therefore, some authors prefer the term *marginalism* for the approach that was introduced almost simultaneously by Stanley Jevons (1835–82) of Manchester, Carl Menger (1840–1921) of Vienna and Léon Walras (1834–1910) of Lausanne. In their use of the marginal principle, the neoclassicists referred to classical rent theory as developed by Ricardo (see Chapter 3), but the term *neoclassical* itself was apparently coined only a generation later, mainly referring to other aspects of marginalism. Thorstein Veblen (an institutionalist whom we will meet in the next chapter) used it in 1900, in a review of *Principles of Economics* (1890), a most influential textbook by the Cambridge economist Alfred Marshall. In Veblen's opinion, Marshall's economics was neo-classical, because it shared a utilitarian base with classical political economy. It should also be noted that, between 1870 and 1900, economists had begun to change the name of their discipline. Jevons stated in the preface to the second edition of his *Theory of Political Economy* (1879) that, in comparison with the first edition of 1871, he had altered 'political economy' to 'the single convenient term *economics*' in the text (see Figure 3).

Marginalism, *utility* and *economics* are indeed three terms that help to show the main parallels *and* differences between classical and neoclassical economic thinking. While classical writers confined their use of the marginal principle largely to the explanation of rent on land and other non-reproducible resources, the neoclassical economists generalized it to a universal principle of rational economic behaviour. Classical writers classified economic agents in terms of their factor contributions to production (labour, land and capital). They set the focus on the supply of goods, driven by the capitalists' search for profit and the concomitant accumulation of capital. In the neoclassical universe, the class divisions were replaced by the simple distinction between

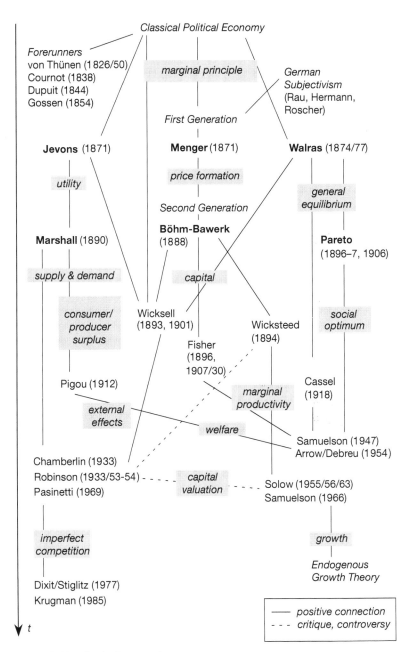

Figure 3 Neoclassical economics

consuming and producing units, nowadays described as households and firms. The utility maximization of households determines their demand for goods and, simultaneously, their supply of factor services to the firms. The firms combine the production factors, produce goods and maximize profits, as in the classical world. But now they do the latter only to provide the households, which own the firms in some way or other, with factor incomes that are eventually spent on consumption. The focus is no longer on capital accumulation as the force that expands the system until a long-run equilibrium is reached in the stationary state. It is shifted onto the proof of the existence, uniqueness and stability of an equilibrium of supply and demand that economic agents in competitive markets will reach at any time, or rather, in no time at all.

The fundamental assumptions of utility and profit maximization were probably one reason why many early neoclassicists were inclined to use mathematics as a tool. Beginning to follow the methods of natural scientists, some of them considered their discipline to be an exact science like mechanics or other parts of physics. A related feature was that the neoclassicists, more than their precursors, tried to distinguish between economic analysis and political recommendations. All this explains the transition from *political economy* to *Economics* as the name of the discipline, present already in Jevons (1879) and fully clear in Marshall (1890).

Another difference is that neoclassical economics predominantly deals with microeconomic questions, that is, the typical behaviour of a single economic unit (household, firm, market), whereas classical thought gave a more prominent place to macroeconomic considerations. Resource allocation by market prices is important in neoclassical as well as in classical analysis. When it comes to the formation of prices, there is, however, a difference between neoclassical and classical thought. Most of the classical economists laid emphasis on the costs of production as determining prices, at least in the long run. Demand could affect market prices only in the short run. Neoclassical economists see prices as determined by the fundamental data of both 'tastes and technology', i.e. by consumer preferences and the available techniques of production.

Neoclassical economics reached another peak with *Foundations of Economic Analysis* (1947) by Paul Samuelson of the Massachusetts Institute of Technology (MIT), and with the works of Kenneth Arrow (b. 1921) of Stanford and Gerard Debreu (1921–2004) of Chicago – notably their joint paper on the *Existence of an Equilibrium for a Competitive Economy* (1954). The neoclassical approach in a broad sense still dominates within practical economic analysis. In the realms of high theory, traditional neoclassical economics has faced strong challenges from game theory, behavioural economics and other new developments in recent decades.

The forerunners

Various elements of marginal analysis existed long before the neoclassical breakthrough. Prominent examples can be found in the works of Johann Heinrich von Thünen (1780–1850), Augustin Cournot (1801–77), Jules Dupuit (1804–66) and Hermann Heinrich Gossen (1810–58). In this chapter we describe some of their main ideas.

Johann Heinrich von Thünen

The learned German landowner von Thünen systematically extended the marginal principle – which Ricardo, in his rent theory, had applied to the production of homogenous goods, such as corn – into a theory of the spatial distribution of the production of heterogeneous goods. Von Thünen developed his location theory within the comprehensive analysis of an isolated economy, *Der isolirte Staat*, whose first volume was published in 1826. The cost of transporting agricultural products to a town increases with the distance from the town, and when the distance is so large that the cost of transportation plus the cost of production exceed the market price of the produce, production will cease at that distance. The important point of the book was thus to show how the cost structure shapes the spatial division of labour.

In the second volume of the *Isolated State* (1850), von Thünen introduced a marginalist argument about labour and capital. More of both on a farm will result in increased produce and increased revenues. However, the costs will increase, too, and finally the point is reached where increased costs will not be covered by increased revenues. The number of workers will, according to von Thünen, continue to grow until the additional revenue produced by the last employed worker equals the wage that he gets during the same period of time. Throughout the book von Thünen applied the principle that profit is maximized when resources are employed to the extent that the cost of the last unit of a resource equals the value of its contribution to output. This typical application of the marginal principle is found also in modern textbooks. Von Thünen used mathematics in a large part of his analysis, and he is often considered to be the first economist who used calculus. The derivatives in a mathematical–economic analysis can often be interpreted as marginal concepts.

Augustin Cournot

There were early marginalists in France, too. The best known are Cournot and Dupuit. We shall focus on Cournot, who gave a mathematical description of the conditions for profit maximum in his *Recherches sur les principes mathématiques de la théorie des richesses* (1838), a book on the mathematics of the theory of wealth. Let us look at his simplest example, where costs are negligible and where the problem for a profit maximizer thus consists of maximizing revenues:

> For convenience in discussion, suppose that a man finds himself proprietor of a mineral spring which has just been found to possess salutary properties possessed by no other. He could doubtless fix the price of a *liter* of this water at 100 francs; but he would soon see by the scant demand, that this is not the way to make the most of his property. He will therefore successively reduce the price of the liter to the point which will give him the greatest possible profit; i.e. if $F(p)$ denotes the law of demand, he will end, after various trials, by adopting the value of p which renders the product $pF(p)$ a maximum, or which is determined by the equation
>
> (1) $F(p) + pF'(p) = 0.$

(Cournot 1963, p. 46)

As the number of demanded and sold litres at a certain price p is shown by the function $F(p)$, the product $pF(p)$ equals total revenues. The price that yields the largest total revenue satisfies the condition that the first-order derivative of total revenue with respect to price equals 0, that is, marginal revenue with respect to price is 0. If the expression for total revenue, $pF(p)$, is differentiated with respect to the price and the result is made equal to 0, equation (1) is obtained.

We can make two comments on Cournot's example. First, he analysed a case of monopoly: the spring possesses 'salutary properties possessed by no other'. To Cournot monopoly was the appropriate starting point of the analysis. Competition with many sellers was a special case that he treated afterwards. Modern neoclassical economics, in contrast, usually considers perfect competition as the general case. Second, we find that, when the maximum conditions are analysed, marginalism results almost naturally. In economic analysis, derivatives are often interpreted as marginal magnitudes. Thus, the value of the derivative $F'(p)$ represents the change in the number of demanded litres that results from a marginal change (1 franc) of the price.

Another remarkable point about Cournot is that he – together with Karl Heinrich Rau (1841) – can be named as inventor of the supply-and-demand diagram in price-quantity space that now populates economics textbooks and often goes under the names *Marshallian cross* or *Marshall's scissors* (see below).

Hermann Heinrich Gossen

In 1854, the Prussian civil servant Gossen published *Die Entwickelung der Gesetze des menschlichen Verkehrs und der daraus fließenden Regeln für menschliches Handeln* (translated as *The Laws of Human Relations and the Rules of Human Action Derived Therefrom*), a book on the determinants and rules of human relations that would become known only after his death. He was both a marginalist and one of the first representatives of the so-called subjective theory of value. The subjective theory of value implies that the value of a thing reflects the utility or enjoyment that the individual experiences by the thing.

Gossen's name has come down to posterity in two of his principles, which are called Gossen's first and second law. Gossen's first law is a version of what is now called the law of diminishing marginal utility, which means that the larger quantity you have of a good, say bread, the less utility or enjoyment you would derive from an additional loaf of bread. Gossen's second law is derived from the first law and the assumption that, due to limited means of payment, the need of a good is not completely saturated. Maximization of utility under a budget restriction implies that the last unit of money spent on different commodities shall give the same additional utility for all commodities. If this is not fulfilled but, for instance, the last pound or dollar spent on bread would increase the consumer's utility less than the alternative spending of that money on apples, the consumer could increase her utility by buying less bread and instead more apples. Maximum utility also implies that the ratio between the marginal utility of a good (i.e. the utility of a marginal unit) and its price is the same for all goods of which a large number is consumed. These are well-known results from elementary microeconomics. Gossen's approach was a bit different from modern texts, but his main results were approximately the same.

Why just 'forerunners'?

Von Thünen, Cournot, Dupuit and Gossen anticipated core ideas of neoclassicism (and so did others whom we cannot mention here). But they did not form a school. With the exception of von Thünen, they were not noticed until after their active time. The reasons are open to speculation. Contacts between economists were more difficult to establish in those times, when transportation and communication were much more costly than now. Furthermore, while contacts within the academic world were relatively close even then, only one of our four forerunners, namely Cournot, was affiliated to a university; and he was a mathematician.

Their style was important, too. Von Thünen's formal style of argumentation provided no easy reading for contemporaneous readers. Similarly, Cournot's and Gossen's mathematical texts were also hard for economists of that time to understand. Dupuit was an engineer and wrote his now well-known articles for an engineering journal which was hardly read by economists.

The neoclassical breakthrough

The breakthrough of neoclassical economics is traditionally dated back to the almost simultaneous publication of Jevons's *The Theory of Political Economy* (1871), Menger's *Grundsätze der Volkswirthschaftslehre* (*Principles of Economics*, 1871) and Walras' *Éléments d'économie politique pure* (*Elements of Pure Economics*, 1874, 1877). We shall follow this convention, even though it is not self-evident, given that marginalist ideas had been around for some while (see the previous section). Moreover, marginalism remained for a long time rather marginal in various countries, such as Germany and the United States, where historical schools and institutionalist ideas ruled the roost (see Chapter 5). In the following we give most space to Jevons and discuss Menger and Walras only insofar as they differ from Jevons in important aspects. We do this in order to keep the book short, not because Menger and Walras are less important.

William Stanley Jevons

Jevons was born in 1835 into a wealthy family in Liverpool. His childhood was overshadowed by illness and death in the family and by the bankruptcy of the family business when he was thirteen. Jevons studied natural sciences in London and worked for a few years as a chemist in Australia before returning in 1859 to London to study logic, philosophy and political economy. In his best-known book, *The Theory of Political Economy* (1871), Jevons was very eager to promote mathematics in economic analysis. Let us look at his arguments:

> It is clear that economics, if it is to be a science at all, must be a mathematical science. There exists much prejudice against attempts to introduce the methods and language of mathematics into any branch of the moral sciences. Many persons seem to think that the physical sciences form the proper sphere of mathematical method, and that the moral sciences demand some other method – I do not know what. My theory of economics, however, is purely mathematical in character. Nay, believing that the quantities with which we deal must be subject to continuous variation, I do not hesitate to use the appropriate branch of mathematical science, involving though it does the fearless consideration of infinitely small quantities. The theory consists in applying the differen-

tial calculus to the familiar notions of wealth, utility, value, demand, supply, capital, interest, labour and all other quantitative notions belonging to the daily operations of industry. As the complete theory of almost every other science involves the use of that calculus, so we cannot have a true theory of economics without its aid.

(p. 78)

After this methodological introduction, Jevons had one chapter on pleasure and pain and one on utility. It is a fundamental question 'how pleasure and pain can be estimated as magnitudes'. Here Jevons referred to the utilitarian Jeremy Bentham (1748–1832), who argued that the quantity of pleasure and pain depends, among other things, on its degrees of intensity, duration, certainty and propinquity (nearness). Jevons concluded:

Pleasure and pain are undoubtedly the ultimate objects of the calculus of economics. To satisfy our wants to the utmost with the least effort – to procure the greatest amount of what is desirable at the expense of the least that is undesirable – in other words, *to maximize pleasure*, is the problem of economics. But it is convenient to transfer our attention as soon as possible to the physical objects or actions which are the source to us of pleasures and pains.

(p. 101)

Discussing the things that are sources of pleasure and pain, Jevons arrived at the concept of utility. He suggested to 'employ the term *utility* to denote the abstract quality whereby an object serves our purposes. . . . Whatever can produce pleasure or prevent pain *may* possess utility' (p. 101). According to Jevons, '[u]tility must be considered as measured by, or even as actually identical with, the addition made to a person's happiness' (p. 106).

It is very important to distinguish between *total utility* and what Jevons called the *final degree of utility*, which we nowadays call *marginal utility*. Sooner or later, marginal utility will decrease in any act of consumption. Discussing decreasing marginal utility, Jevons commented upon what in an earlier chapter we called the paradox of value:

The final degree of utility is that function upon which the theory of economics will be found to turn. Economists, generally speaking, have failed to discriminate between this function and the total utility, and from this confusion has arisen much perplexity. Many commodities which are most useful to us are esteemed and desired but little. We cannot live without water, and yet in ordinary circumstances we set no value on it. Why is this? Simply because we usually have so much of it that its final degree of utility is reduced nearly to zero. We enjoy, every day, the almost infinite utility of water, but then we do not need to consume more than we have. Let the supply run short by drought, and we begin to feel the higher degrees of utility, of which we think but little at other times.

(p. 111)

The theory of utility leads to a theory of exchange and a theory of prices, where Jevons deduced equilibrium conditions which are now well-known. He began with a discussion of the notion of value, which he found ambiguous and therefore inexpedient. Instead, he preferred the term *ratio of exchange* which, however, did not restrain him from using the word *value* now and then.

The analysis is based on several specified conditions. One is that there is a market, defined as two or more persons dealing in two or more commodities. The traders in the market have perfect knowledge of the conditions of supply and demand and the ratios of exchange. The commodities are homogeneous and completely divisible. The core message is formulated in the following way:

> The keystone of the whole theory of exchange, and of the principal theory of economics, lies in this proposition – *The ratio of exchange of any two commodities will be the reciprocal of the ratio of the final degree of utility of the quantities of commodity available for consumption after the exchange is completed.*

(p. 139)

This means, for instance, that if the ratio of exchange is ten pounds of corn for one pound of beef, for a person in equilibrium the utility of an additional pound of beef is ten times greater than the utility of an extra pound of corn. If the latter condition were not fulfilled – if, say, the utility of an extra pound of beef were only five times larger than the utility of an extra pound of corn – it would be advantageous to the person to acquire more corn at the exchange ratio ten pounds of corn for one pound of beef. The marginal utility of corn would decrease and the marginal utility of beef would increase after such an exchange. A utility-maximizing individual would continue exchanging until the ratio of the final degree of utility was equal to the reciprocal of the ratio of exchange.

Jevons rejected the labour theory of value. Antiquities and similar things have a price which is fairly independent of the amount of labour invested in their production. Goods produced in the past and present, such as cotton, corn and iron, have fluctuating prices in the present and the future, even if the labour input is constant. 'The fact is, that *labour once spent has no influence on the future value of any article*: it is gone and lost for ever. In commerce bygones are for ever bygones; and we are always starting clear at each moment, judging the values of things with a view to future utility' (p. 186). Jevons's final position is, however, less distant from the labour theory of value than the passage above may indicate:

> But though labour is never the cause of value, it is in a large proportion of cases the determining circumstance, and in the following way: *Value depends solely on the final degree of utility. How can we vary this degree of utility? – By having more or less of the commodity to consume. And how shall we get more or less of it? – By spending more or less labour in obtaining a supply.* According to this view, then, there are two steps between labour and value. Labour affects supply, and supply affects the degree of utility, which governs value, or the ratio of exchange.
>
> (pp. 186–7)

What determines the value of labour? Jevons connected the first and the last point. He maintained that the value of labour must be determined by the value of the produce, not the value of the produce by that of the labour. In sum, we can say that Jevons emphasized utility in his theoretical work, but that labour and production were not completely neglected.

Carl Menger

Jevons's *Theory of Political Economy* appeared in 1871. In the same year Menger published his *Grundsätze (Principles of Economics)* in Vienna. With this he became the founder of the Austrian version of the neoclassical school. Representatives of the modern neo-Austrian school are reluctant to classify Menger as a neoclassicist (see Chapter 7); but he clearly contributed to the rise of neoclassical economics by inspiring leading thinkers in the later generations.

While Jevons and Walras considered themselves to be innovators or even revolutionaries in economic thought, Menger did not claim to be more than a reformer of nineteenth century German economic thought. Karl Heinrich Rau (1792–1870), Friedrich B. W. von Hermann (1795–1868) and Wilhelm Roscher (1817–94) had laid the foundations for a subjective theory of value. They had set the focus on what the individual thinks and feels, objecting to the classical theory of prices based on the costs of production, and attempting to create a unifom price theory that applies to both consumption goods and factors of production.

Menger differed from Jevons and Walras insofar as he presented his marginalist ideas without mathematical formulas or diagrams. He discussed needs and satisfaction, illustrating the marginal principle in a table where declining numbers show the additional satisfaction from marginal units of different commodities. He thus put forward the hypothesis of decreasing marginal utility, though without using that term. Maximum total satisfaction requires that the last unit of money spent on each good makes the same contribution to total utility. Menger was not, however, very clear on this point. In Menger we find also elements that gained prominence in various streams of economic thinking only much later. He emphasised the role of information in the economy, and he analysed the time-structure of production, which became important for the development of the Austrian theory of capital (discussed later in this chapter). Menger regarded economic life, and in particular market processes, as phenomena where equilibrium did not prevail in reality. He described price formation as a struggle, in which a unique market(-clearing) price is not normally achieved.

Menger also wrote on methodological questions, and became one of the main combatants in the famous *Methodenstreit*, the controversy about methods of economic research that raged in the German language area in the 1880s. He argued that research should concentrate on developing pure economics by way of deducing 'exact economic laws' from assumptions about human behaviour and about predetermined data. His deductive method stood in contrast to the inductive method of the then dominant historical school, which maintained that historical data should form the basis for seeking recurrent regularities. We will return to the *Methodenstreit* in Chapter 5.

Léon Walras

The Frenchman Walras never obtained an academic position in his native country. As a young man, he failed twice to gain admittance to the respected *École polytechnique*, and he had a number of jobs as a journalist and an accountant before being offered a professorship in Lausanne in Switzerland in 1870, which he held until 1892. In Lausanne, however, Walras gained great respect. In the early twentieth century, the term *Lausanne school* was frequently used to denote both Walras and his successor Vilfredo Pareto (1848–1923) and the mathematical analysis of general equilibrium that they argued for.

Walras differed from Jevons and Menger in the sense that he developed the idea of a general equilibrium of supply and demand in all markets that can be consistently captured by a system of equations. Walras' most important work, *Éléments* (of Pure Economics), was published in two parts in 1874 and 1877, and later in several revised editions. In his system of equations, Walras treated prices and quantities as endogenous variables, i.e. as variables whose values are determined within the system. His theory includes demand equations, equations in which costs are set equal to prices, supply equations for factor services, and equations for technical coefficients. In equilibrium, the prices of the goods are proportional to the marginal utilities for each consumer. One of the goods is treated as *numéraire*, the unit of account. The number of equations is equal to the number of endogenous variables, and under certain assumptions the values of the endogenous variables can be determined. The prices and quantities determined in this way can be interpreted as equilibrium values. Walras imagined that the economy may achieve the equilibrium state by way of a *tâtonnement*, a process like the bidding at an auction.

In Walras' system it becomes apparent that, if one has information about all markets except one, and if none of these other markets is characterized by excess demand, it can be concluded that there is no excess demand on the remaining market either. This has been called *Walras' law*. The logic behind it became crucial for the study of general equilibrium. The Swedish economist Gustav Cassel was an important disseminator of Walras' ideas through his *Theoretische Sozialökonomie* (*Theory of Social Economy*, 1918) – even though, strangely enough, he failed to give Walras due credit. Cassel nevertheless inspired other economists to produce mathematical proofs of the existence, uniqueness and stability of a general equilibrium in competitive markets. When Arrow and Debreu achieved this in the 1950s, they seemed to have fulfilled the old dream of economists – in particular Smith and Walras – to show rigorously that there was a hidden, but socially desirable order in the apparently chaotic transactions of self-interested individuals who compete in a system of markets.

Why the neoclassical breakthrough?

Several reasons for the marginalist breakthrough are put forward in the literature. One concerns the decline of the classical labour theory of value. In the second half of the nineteenth century it had been abandoned together with the wage-fund doctrine. This classical doctrine (with physiocratic roots) claimed that the amount of capital available for wage payments is essentially fixed, such that wages have to fall when the population grows and vice versa. This could be a reasonable approach in an agricultural economy where the crops in autumn determine the provisions of the following year. The wage-fund doctrine was incompatible with utility-based theories of prices and factor supplies. It has also been speculated that marginal utility theory was a product of the *Zeitgeist*, the spirit of the time within philosphy and the social sciences. Hedonism, the philosophy of maximizing pleasure, was in fact *en vogue* in England in the mid-nineteenth century and it apparently influenced Jevons, but it is difficult to find such influences on Menger and Walras.

A third reason that has been suggested is the type of institutional changes in the economy that occurred at the time when neoclassical economics made its breakthrough. Unlike classical thought, marginal utility theory focuses on the consuming individual. This may be linked to the fact that the consumers in the high years of industrialization became more clearly separated from production than at the times of Smith and Ricardo.

According to another argument, the neoclassical school arose as a bourgeois reaction against Marxism. This is, however, hardly compatible with the chronology. Jevons presented the essence of his theory at the British Association for the Advancement of Science as early as 1862, five years before Marx published his *Capital* (in German; the English translation came only in 1887). Neither Menger nor Walras seem to have been aware of Marx's economic writings when developing their ideas. Consequently, marginalism can hardly have arisen in reaction to them, but it is of course possible that Marxism influenced its later propagation.

The second generation

A number of persons who made lasting contributions form the second generation of neoclassical economists. The group includes the Britons Alfred Marshall (1842–1924), Francis Ysidro Edgeworth (1845–1926), Philip Henry Wicksteed (1844–1927) and Arthur Cecil Pigou (1877–1959), the Austrians Eugen von Böhm-Bawerk (1851–1914) and Friedrich von Wieser (1851–1926), the Italian Vilfredo Pareto (1848–1923), the Americans John Bates Clark (1847–1938) and Irving Fisher (1867–1947), and the Swedes Knut Wicksell (1851–1926) and Gustav Cassel (1866–1945). These economists deepened and extended the analysis, introducing and popularizing many of the concepts that today's students meet – for instance, the indifference curve and the contract curve (Edgeworth), purchasing power parity (Cassel), supply and demand schedules, consumer and producer surplus (both Marshall), the Wicksell effect, Pigovian tax, and Pareto efficency.

Even if some extensions of the marginal approach to the explanation of production can be discerned in earlier neoclassical works, it was only the second-generation neoclassicists who analysed the production or supply side as thoroughly as the consumption or demand side. They linked the theory of income formation more closely to the theory of production again. Some of the second-generation neoclassicists assumed that the relation between the input of different factors of production and the output can be described by a production function which in mathematical terms is homogeneous of the first degree. Together with the assumption that each factor of production is paid according to the value of its marginal product, this implies that the whole produce is distributed by a uniform principle. An early example of such an analysis is given by Wicksteed in his *An Essay on the Co-ordination of the Laws of Distribution* (1894), another is provided by Clark in *The Distribution of Wealth* (1899) and a third by Wicksell in his *Lectures on Political Economy* (1901).

Alfred Marshall and Arthur Cecil Pigou

Alfred Marshall is often considered the foremost neoclassicist of the second generation. He was born in London in 1842 as the son of a humble clerk in the Bank of England. At school and as a student at the University of Cambridge he demonstrated an aptitude for mathematics, and even taught mathematics in the 1860s. In the mid-1860s he became more interested in philosophy, psychology and political economy. He was appointed lecturer in the moral sciences in 1868, but – due to the celibacy rules of the time – he had to leave the University of Cambridge nine years later, when he married his former student Mary Paley. Together with her he published the textbook *Economics of Industry* in 1879. After shorter positions in Bristol and Oxford, Marshall returned to Cambridge, where he held the chair of political economy from 1885 until 1908. In 1890, he published his *magnum opus*, *Principles of Economics*, which appeared in eight editions during his lifetime. A second volume on applied economics was planned, but Marshall never managed to complete it. Instead he produced a couple of companion volumes, such as *Industry and Trade* (1919) and *Money, Credit and Commerce* (1923).

Marshall's main contribution was within microeconomic theory. Like Jevons, but in contrast to Walras, he especially promoted the partial equilibrium approach, i.e. the analysis of an equilibrium in a single market, rather than general equilibrium in a system of markets. Unlike Jevons and Menger, who emphasized the demand side, Marshall gave the demand side and the supply side equal weight. We may quote a passage from *Principles of Economics* that is an example of this kind of analysis:

> When therefore the amount produced (in a unit of time) is such that the demand price [i.e. the highest price the consumers are willing to pay] is greater than the supply price [the lowest price the sellers are willing to accept], then sellers receive more than is sufficient to make it worth their while to bring goods to market to that amount; and there is at work an active force tending to increase the amount brought forward for sale. On the other hand, when the amount produced is such that the demand price is less than the supply price, sellers receive less than is sufficient to make it worth their while to bring goods to market on that scale; so that those who were just on the margin of doubt as to whether to go on producing are decided not to do so, and there is an active force at work tending to diminish the amount brought forward for sale. When the demand price is equal to the supply price, the amount produced has no tendency either to be increased or to be diminished; it is in equilibrium.
>
> When demand and supply are in equilibrium, the amount of the commodity which is being produced in a unit of time may be called the

equilibrium-amount, and the price at which it is being sold may be called the *equilibrium-price.*

(p. 345)

Marshall illustrated his reasoning with the now common diagram (see Figure 4) showing the quantity of the good on the horizontal axis, price on the vertical axis, a downward-sloping demand curve, an upward-sloping supply curve, and equilibrium price and equilibrium amount (quantity) given by the intersection of the two curves. The supply curve is based on 'cost of production', and the demand curve is based on 'utility'. Marshall compares the curves with the two blades of a pair of scissors: 'We might as reasonably dispute whether it is the upper or the under blade of a pair of scissors that cuts a piece of paper, as whether value is governed by utility or cost of production' (p. 348). Figure 4 shows the now conventional form of market diagrams that have frequently been called 'Marshall's scissors' or 'the Marshallian cross' – even though the concept dates back to Cournot (1838) and Rau (1841); (see above).

Marshall's way of doing economic analysis and writing economic texts followed a tradition that has been described as influenced by physics, a very prestigious science at the end of the nineteenth century (Jevons and Walras were other representatives of this tradition). But to Marshall this approach seems to have been a sacrifice, required to facilitate understanding and acceptance among economists. At several occasions he suggested instead biology as the ideal model. In the preface of the eighth edition of the *Principles* (1920) he explained:

> The Mecca of the economist lies in economic biology rather than in economic dynamics. But biological conceptions are more complex than those of mechanics; a volume on Foundations must therefore give a relatively large place to mechanical analogies; and frequent use is made of the term 'equilibrium', which suggests something of statical analogy.
>
> (p. xiv)

Marshall's *Principles of Economics* was for several decades the most important book in the propagation of economics in the English language area. Naturally, some of its concepts have become common property. They are now used without any indication of their origin. One is the concept of elasticity of demand, which Marshall defines first for a person and then for a market. The elasticity, defined as the percentage change in quantity of demand divided by the percentage change in price, may be different for different levels of the price, different classes of the population and different kinds of goods, all described by vivid examples.

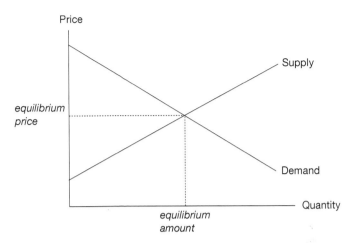

Figure 4 Market diagram

Another legacy of Marshall is the concept of consumer surplus (in his diction 'consumer's surplus' or, in the first edition of the *Principles*, 'consumer's rent'). For an individual, the consumer surplus from buying a thing is measured as the 'excess of the price which he would be willing to pay rather than go without the thing, over that which he actually does pay' (p. 124). It can be defined for a market, too. Marshall states that in a figure with a demand curve, consumer surplus equals the area delimited by the demand curve, the price axis, and a horizontal line from the actual price to the demand curve.

By analogy, Marshall defines producer surplus as an area delimited by the supply curve, the price axis, and a horizontal line from the actual price to the supply curve. This concept is tricky as the determination of the supply curve is more complex and depends on the time horizon. In a simplified version, both types of Marshall's concept of surplus can be illustrated by Figure 5.

Marshall also introduced the now indispensable concept of the representative firm and conceived it 'in a sense [as] an average firm' (p. 318). His concern for the supply side manifests itself in his discussion of equilibrium, where the time period is crucial. He considered three main cases, but noted that they 'merge into one another by imperceptible degrees' (p. 330). The first is the very short period, a single day, when 'the supply is limited to the stores which happen to be at hand' (p. 330). The second is the case when some costs of production may change and cause variation in supply. The third is the case of the very long period, when even 'the cost of producing the

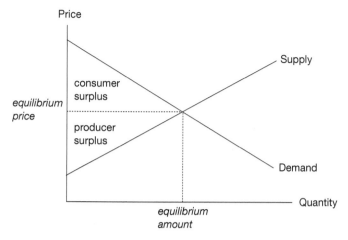

Figure 5 Marshall's concepts of consumer and producer surplus

labour and the material things required for producing the commodity' may change, i.e. when costs that are fixed in a shorter period have become variable.

Marshall was succeeded in his Cambridge chair in 1908 by Arthur Cecil Pigou. It was not only a formal succession. Pigou spread Marshallian economics by way of his lectures, and many of his own writings were in the Marshallian tradition. Among his works are *Wealth and Welfare* (1912) which was published in several editions under different titles. Pigou introduced the distinction between private and social marginal costs and benefits as well as the concept of external effects. To make private and social marginal costs or benefits coincide in order to increase overall efficiency, Pigou suggested government measures, such as taxes and subsidies. The *Pigovian tax* is now a familiar concept.

Vilfredo Pareto

As mentioned before, Léon Walras was succeeded as professor in Lausanne by Vilfredo Pareto. Pareto was born in Paris in the year of the February Revolution, 1848, as the son of a simple French woman and an Italian marquis. The family moved to Italy in 1852, where Pareto was brought up. He studied classics and engineering, and became proficient in mathematics. The science of engineering made him acquainted with the concept of equilibrium in mechanics, which obviously came to influence his economic analysis.

In the 1870s and 1880s Pareto held different positions in business and industry. At the same time he took part in the public debate and wrote a lot in the spirit of liberalism. In 1890 he met the Italian economist Maffeo Pantaleoni (1857–1924), who persuaded him to study Walras. Thus, Pareto was in his early forties when he began to study economics seriously. He advanced rapidly, and when Walras was to leave his chair in Lausanne, Pantaleoni recommended Pareto as successor. In 1893 he became associate and in 1894 full professor in Lausanne. Around the turn of the century he left liberalism. Most of his later writings belong to sociology rather than economics, and some of his sociological ideas attracted the Italian fascists.

Pareto's textbook *Cours d'économie politique* was published in three volumes in 1896–7. It was based on his lecture notes, and manifested an endeavour to apply the thinking of natural sciences to economics. But his most famous economic publication is his *Manual of Political Economy* (1906), a foundational work in the history of welfare economics and general equilibrium theory. Pareto was critical of the lack of rigour in the use of the concept of utility by earlier economists. Furthermore, he pointed out that utility had a different meaning in political economy as compared to everyday language. Pareto points at morphine, which 'is not useful, in the ordinary sense of the word, since it is harmful to the morphine addict; on the other hand it is *useful* to him, even though it is unhealthful, because it satisfies one of his wants' (Pareto 1971, p. 111). Pareto therefore used the word *ophelimity* instead of utility; morphine would give the addict ophelimity.

Pareto's name is probably best remembered because of the concept of *Pareto optimality*, or, as it often called now, *Pareto efficiency* – a criterion for the optimal state of an economy that, in a similar fashion, had actually been developed by Edgeworth a few years earlier. Pareto himself talked about *maximum ophelimity*, and defined it in the following way:

> We will say that the members of a collectivity enjoy *maximum ophelimity* in a certain position when it is impossible to find a way of moving from that position very slightly in such a manner that the ophelimity enjoyed by each of the individuals of that collectivity increases or decreases.
>
> (Pareto 1971, p. 261)

This is only slightly different from modern textbook definitions. Pareto presents maximum ophelimity as a property of equilibrium. That is what has later been termed the first theorem of welfare economics: a competitive equilibrium is a Pareto optimum.

Foundations of the neoclassical theory of capital

A special feature of economic thinking in the late nineteenth and early twentieth century is the view on capital, elaborated especially by the Austrian Eugen von Böhm-Bawerk in his *Positive Theory of Capital* (1889) and refined by the Swede Knut Wicksell in his *Value, Capital and Rent* (1893) and *Lectures on Political Economy* (1901), the American Irving Fisher in *The Nature of Capital and Income* (1906), *The Rate of Interest* (1907) and *The Theory of Interest* (1930), and various others. Prior to Böhm-Bawerk the American John Bates Clark had published *Capital and its Earnings* in 1888, but Fisher was more inspired by Böhm-Bawerk and the Scottish-born John Rae (1796–1872). At the core of the theory of capital was the ancient issue of the rate of interest (see Chapter 2), although now the focus was set on its origin, its economic explanation and its systematic relationship with capital accumulation rather than its moral aspects. The theory of capital was until, say, the 1970s, a fairly well-defined field of economic theory. In the realms of neoclassical economics, however, it is no longer a field that generates a discernible literature of its own. Some would say it has been absorbed by growth theory and general micro- and macroeconomics. Others would say it is stuck in a dead-end street.

Böhm-Bawerk was born in Brno in 1851 as the youngest son of an ennobled civil servant. He was professor first in Innsbruck in 1880 and from 1905 in Wien, but in between he was employed in the ministry of finance and was during some periods minister of finance. Wicksell was born in Stockholm, in the same year as Böhm-Bawerk. But, while the Austrian was well established in the high society of his country, the Swede had the reputation of an *enfant terrible*, a radical (though non-Marxist) iconoclast who defied the Church, the military and everyone whose opinion he did not share. In personal encounters he nevertheless came across as a most amiable and humble man. As a student in Uppsala, Wicksell caused a scandal when he pleaded in a public lecture for birth control. As a 57-year-old professor, who by then was respected as a great economist, he spent two months in prison for 'reviling and mocking God's holy word in such circumstances as to cause general offence'. After protracted studies in a number of subjects, and a licentiate's degree in mathematics, Wicksell had begun studying economics only when he was in his mid-thirties – evidently because the Uppsala economist David Davidson had criticized him for insufficient economic knowledge during the population debate. After many years of trouble with the moral authorities, Wicksell was eventually appointed as professor at Lund University in 1901. The 1890s were nevertheless his most productive period, in which he published great contributions to the theories of capital, public finance and money.

Fisher was born in upstate New York in 1867 and affiliated with Yale University during his whole career, serving as full professor from 1898 to 1935. He was similar to Wicksell in at least four respects. First, he wrote copiously, often in a provocative way, in many diverse areas of economics as well as outside economics, for instance about eugenics, temperance or vegetarianism. Second, he considered it an important duty to educate the general public. Third, he had a solid mathematical background. Fourth, both Wicksell and Fisher explicitly refer to Böhm-Bawerk's work as the foundation upon which they build. In relation to Böhm-Bawerk, they modify and reject different points. Böhm-Bawerk's and Wicksell's approach is sometimes called the Austrian theory of capital, in which time plays a key role.

Böhm-Bawerk regarded interest as an agio which appears when present and future goods are exchanged. When present and future goods are valued at the same time, present goods are as a general rule subjectively more valuable than future goods. The interest rate will reflect that difference as a compensatory payment. Böhm-Bawerk adduced three causes for a positive interest rate. First, in a growing economy the supply of goods will be greater in the future and their marginal utility consequently lower. Second, there is a characteristic of human beings such that 'we feel less concerned about future sensations of joy and sorrow simply because they do lie in the future'. Böhm-Bawerk's third cause is related to the production side: 'time-consuming roundabout methods of production are more productive.' Instead of catching fish immediately with the hands, it is more productive first to spend some time constructing a fishing-rod or a net.

Knut Wicksell emphasized the production side. Capital goods are produced by labour and land (and perhaps other capital goods) which have been put into the production process a shorter or a longer time before output is received. Thus: 'Capital is saved-up labour and saved-up land. Interest is the difference between the marginal productivity of saved-up labour and land and of current labour and land' (*Lectures I*, p. 154). We will turn to Wicksell's contributions to public finance and monetary theory in the further course of this book.

In Irving Fisher's approach, the willingness and the possibility to reallocate income between different periods of time provides the setting for the analysis of capital formation. This is obvious from the full title of his 1930 book *The Theory of Interest As Determined by Impatience To Spend Income and Opportunity To Invest It*. The invested income will be paid back with an addition in the future, provided that not too much is invested. In equilibrium, such addition to marginal invested income is an expression of the investor's 'impatience'. We will meet Fisher again, in the context of monetary theory, in Chapter 6.

Imperfect competition, growth and capital controversies

Neoclassical models have usually been based on one of the two extremes of market forms, *perfect competition* and *monopoly* – mostly the former. However, in the 1930s much attention was paid to intermediate forms like monopolistic competition and oligopoly. The key contributions to this research were two books that appeared simultaneously, but independently of each other: *The Theory of Monopolistic Competition* (1933) by Edward H. Chamberlin (1899–1967) of Harvard, and *Economics of Imperfect Competition* (1933) by Joan Robinson (1903–83) of Cambridge. It is not evident, though, that these two writers should be labelled as neoclassicists. Joan Robinson, at any rate, was later in her life very critical of essential parts of neoclassical thought. We mention these works nevertheless because marginal concepts, such as marginal revenue and marginal cost, play an important role, especially in Robinson's book.

These contributions from the 1930s were rather neglected for a long time. It was only in the late 1970s that interest in imperfect competition was revived by Avinash Dixit (b. 1944) and Joseph Stiglitz (b. 1944), both then at Princeton, and Paul Krugman (b. 1953), then at MIT. It became, for instance, evident that important conclusions about welfare and trade policy had to be modified if the assumption of imperfect competition was introduced. The case for *laissez faire* became less obvious. The Dixit-Stiglitz (1977) model of monopolistic competition has become a workhorse model in industrial economics, international trade theory, geographical economics, macro-economics and many other fields. Despite various strong restrictions, it has many features – such as price-setting and positive profits of firms, or consumer's love for variety – that provide more scope for analysing the real world than the perfect competition model.

In the 1950s, neoclassical growth models came into vogue. The point of departure was an article in 1956 by Robert Solow (b. 1924) of MIT. Solow's model was based on an aggregate production function and built on the assumptions that a certain proportion of total income is saved, that the labour force grows independently of other factors, and that technical progress is exogenous, i.e. occurs independently of capital accumulation and changes in the labour supply. The key attribute of Solow's model is its demonstration that the economic growth process is stable. Capital accumulation converges towards a long-term steady state equilibrium that is determined exogenously by the growth rates of population and productivity – and thus, implicitly, by the fundamental data of neoclassical economics, consumer preferences and the state of technology. This implies that saving and capital accumulation does not matter for growth in the long run: *per capita* income will remain constant in the steady state; it will grow only if there is exogenous technical progress.

Solow's growth model gained great popularity in the 1950s and 1960s, when many former British and French colonies gained independence and economic development was set on top of the agenda. The charm of the model lay in two optimistic predictions about the economic development of relatively poorer countries. First, as their capital stock is comparatively small, they have the potential to catch up on the richer countries: when climbing up on a well-behaved neoclassical production function (which is concave), the growth rates are highest when the capital stock is smallest. Second, poorer countries can benefit from a technology transfer from the richer countries without much extra investment. Applied to the growth problems of developing countries, however, this kind of highly aggregated model may have resulted in too much concentration on capital and technology transfer, and too little attention to institutional factors and short-run disturbances. In the 1970s and early 1980s, the interest in such models decreased, and growth theory lost prestige. It increased again in the late 1980s and early 1990s when models of endogenous growth were developed, in which technical progress (and hence productivity and output growth) is generated within the model. The main contributors to this literature were Robert Lucas (b. 1937), Paul Romer (b. 1955), then both of Chicago, and Philippe Aghion (b. 1956), then at MIT and Oxford, in cooperation with Peter Howitt (b. 1946), then at Western Ontario.

However, the key assumption of a macroeconomic production function – in particular the notion of a well-defined value of an aggregate capital stock – had been challenged in the so-called Cambridge controversies on capital theory that raged from the 1950s until the 1970s. The name of the controversies is explained by the fact that several of the critics of neoclassical capital theory – most prominently Joan Robinson, Piero Sraffa and Luigi Pasinetti (b. 1930) – were affiliated with Cambridge University in England, while the neoclassical camp – mainly represented by Paul Samuelson and Robert Solow – had their base at MIT in Cambridge, Massachusetts. The controversy revolved around a circularity problem in the neoclassical theory of capital and interest that had, in fact, been known since the days of Wicksell: in a world with heterogenous goods (a possibility that should not be ignored in macroeconomic models) the quantity of aggregate capital invested in production must be defined in terms of its value, i.e. a price sum, for whose determination the price(s) needs to be given; in the logic of neoclassical economics, however, part of the price of capital services, the rate of interest, is determined by the marginal productivity and relative scarcity of aggregate capital. Thus, in order to determine the rate of interest, one must know the value of aggregate capital, which cannot be determined without knowing the rate of interest.

The Cambridge controversies revealed that theoretical problems easily appear when the value of capital is used as an argument in a production function. It also made clear that it may be impossible to maintain that one method of production is unequivocally more capital-intensive than another method. This, in turn, means that traditional neoclassical conclusions, such as the claim that a higher rate of interest makes it profitable to use less capital-intensive methods of production, become questionable. The representatives of neoclassicism have not denied the logic of the criticism of neoclassical capital (and growth) theory, but have reduced it dismissively to the question of which approximations are generally acceptable in order to make a problem manageable.

The Cambridge controversies over capital theory were not the only challenges to neoclassical economics. We have mentioned the *Methodenstreit* between Menger and protagonists of the German historical school, to which we will turn in the next chapter. The development of Keynesian and other monetary macroeconomics, which we will discuss in Chapter 6, was another great challenge to neoclassical thinking. Finally, it should be noted that it has become rather difficult to provide a clear and universally accepted definition of what neoclassical economics is nowadays, even though – or perhaps because – it remains the dominant mode of thinking in economics. Neoclassical elements of analysis are now applied in practically all fields of economic research, and beyond that in social, political and psychological research – not to speak of biology, one of the disciplines that used to be a role model for early neoclassicists. But the core principles of neoclassical economics are also critically examined and modified in various new approaches, if not outright rejected in heterodox theories. We will turn to some of these developments in Chapter 7.

References

Arrow, Kenneth and Debreu, Gerard (1954) Existence of an Equilibrium of a Competitive Economy, *Econometrica* 22: 265–90.

Blaug, Mark, (1985) *Economic Theory in Retrospect*. Cambridge: Cambridge University Press.

Busino, Giovanni (1987) Pareto, Vilfredo. *The New Palgrave: A Dictionary of Economics*. London: Macmillan.

Cohen, Avi and Harcourt, Geoffrey (2003) Whatever Happened to the Cambridge Capital Controversies?, *Journal of Economic Perspectives* 17: 199–214.

Cournot, Augustin (1963) [1838] *Researches into the Mathematical Principles of the Theory of Wealth*, translation of French edition. Homewood, IL: Richard D. Irwin, Inc.

Dixit, Avinash and Stiglitz, Joseph E. (1977) Monopolisitic Competition and Optimum Product Diversity, *American Economic Review* 67: 297–308.

Groenewegen, Peter (1995) *A Soaring Eagle: Alfred Marshall 1842–1924*. Hants and Brookfield: Edward Elgar.

Hennings, Klaus and Samuels, Warren (eds) (1990) *Neoclassical Economic Theory, 1870 to 1930.* Boston, Dordrecht, London: Kluwer Academic Publishers.

Humphrey, Thomas M. (1992) Marshallian Cross Diagrams and Their Uses Before Alfred Marshall: The Origins of Supply and Demand Geometry, *Federal Reserve Bank of Richmond Economic Review* 78: 3–23.

Jevons, W. Stanley (1970) [1871, 1879] *The Theory of Political Economy.* Harmondsworth: Penguin Books.

Marshall, Alfred (1961) [1890] *Principles of Economics* (9th variorum edition). London: Macmillan.

Pareto, Vilfredo (1971) [1906] *Manual of Political Economy*, translation of French edition by Ann S. Schwier. London: Macmillan.

Roll, Eric (1973) *A History of Economic Thought* (4th ed.). London: Faber and Faber.

Sandelin, Bo (1989) Wicksell's Wicksell Effect, the Price Wicksell Effect, and the Real Wicksell Effect. In Barber, William J. (ed.) *Perspectives on the History of Economic Thought*, vol. VI. Aldershot: Edward Elgar.

Spiegel, Henry William (1971) *The Growth of Economic Thought.* Durham, NC: Duke University Press.

Stigler, George J. (1941) *Production and Distribution Theories: The Formative Period.* New York: Macmillan.

Thünen, Johann Heinrich von (1966) [1826, 1850] *Isolated State: An English Edition of Der isolierte Staat*, translation by Carla Wartenberg. Oxford: Pergamon Press.

Tobin, James (1987) Fisher, Irving. *The New Palgrave: A Dictionary of Economics.* London: Macmillan.

Veblen, Thorstein (1900) The Preconceptions of Economic Science, part III, *Quarterly Journal of Economics* 14: 240–69.

Whitaker, John K. (1987) Marshall, Alfred. *The New Palgrave: A Dictionary of Economics.* London: Macmillan.

5 Historical schools and institutionalism

One of the characteristics of classical and neoclassical economic thought is the quest for universal laws and principles of economic behaviour. Another characteristic is the use of the deductive method, the reasoning in models that ignore institutional and historical details in order to reduce complex reality to its perceived economic essence. A third characteristic is the atomistic approach by which aggregate production is explained as the beneficial outcome of seemingly anarchic transactions between entirely self-interested individuals.

Ever since the early nineteenth century, economists of various origins have reacted critically to this triad, arguing that the economic laws and principles of the (neo)classical doctrines apply, at best, under specific historic circumstances. These critics have pointed out that those doctrines presuppose institutional frameworks which may correspond to a certain stage in the development of some nations, but not of others. Such 'relativist' reasoning was most distinctly developed by the nineteenth century historical schools of Germany and by American institutionalism in the early twentieth century. Members of both groups founded important associations, edited influential journals and engaged in heated controversies about methods and norms. As we will see, however, historicist and institutionalist ideas were not confined to Germany and the USA. Moreover, the relationship between the relativist approaches and the (neo)classical doctrines was not all critical; there was some cross-fertilization, too (see Figure 6).

The forerunners

To begin with, the label *historical school* denoted a movement in the study of German law, early in the nineteenth century. Its members rejected the concept of natural law and emphasized the national law heritage as expression of the will of the people (*Volksgeist*). The turn towards a romantic notion of the nation soon found its counterpart in economic thinking.

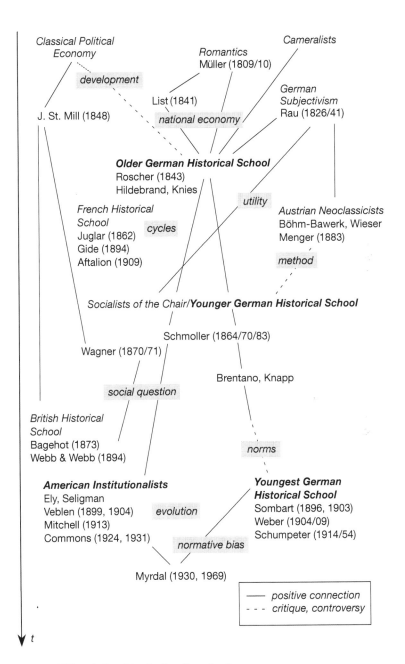

Figure 6 Historical and institutionalist schools

Cameralists, subjectivists and romantics

The eighteenth-century German mercantilists, who are also known as *cameralists* (see Chapter 2), paved the way for the historical school by emphasizing the role of the state as the primary economic subject. Many of the central issues of the cameralists' works – such as public finance and administration, and population growth – came to be the focus of historicist writers in the late nineteenth century.

Another group of forerunners were the *German subjectivists*, notably the Heidelberg professor Rau (see Chapter 4). Various German historicists, in particular Knies and Wagner, based their writings on Rau's *Grundsätze der Volkswirthschaftslehre* (4th ed., 1841 and after). The title of Rau's book is echoed in Menger's *magnum opus*, and his concepts of utility, demand and supply came to influence the Austrian neoclassicists through the teachings of the older historical school (see below). Rau also emphasized the importance of historical investigation for the understanding of the present economy.

The *romantic economists* were a group of writers who rejected the 'vulgar materialism' and rationalism of classical political economy, in particular its quantification of value in terms of physical labour. They suggested that value should instead be defined in terms of the 'moral contribution' of the citizen to the 'organism of the state', the political entity of the nation. The economists were part of the greater romantic movement that in the early nineteenth century pervaded German literature, art and philosophy, and spread to other countries – for example to Britain, where Thomas Carlyle (1795–1881) and John Ruskin (1819–1900) were prominent representatives. The movement can be understood as a reaction against French Enlightenment and Napoleonic armies, British industrialism and trade dominance, and the political fragmentation of Germany, which at that time was divided in many small states.

The Austrian diplomat Adam Müller (1779–1829) was one of the most prominent writers in the romantic tradition. He criticized physiocratic and classical thinking for its bloodless abstractions and condemned the destructive power of mercantile competition and industrialism. He pleaded for a holistic view of society and for the return to a corporative and authoritarian order of the state as it had existed in the Middle Ages. Müller's ideas may seem outlandish now, but they exerted some influence on various movements of economic nationalism and anti-industrialism in the nineteenth and twentieth centuries.

Friedrich List

List (1789–1846) does not easily fit any pattern. He started as an office clerk who made a career in the state bureaucracy of Württemberg, a small state in

South Germany, and was appointed to a professorship in public administration at Tübingen University. Turning rebel against bureaucracy and trade barriers within Germany, he was dismissed. After further conflicts with the state government, he was even sentenced to jail and forced to emigrate to the United States, where he made a career as a mining and railways entrepreneur – only to return to Germany some years later as American consul. List propagated free trade and railway networks within Germany and educational external tariffs to protect its fledgling industries. His life ended tragically in financial and political failure, but he has been posthumously hailed as a progenitor of German unification and pioneer of development economics.

In 1841 List published his main work, *Das nationale System der Politischen Oekonomie*. Together with Rau's aforementioned *Volkswirtschaftslehre*, this book was influential in renaming the discipline as 'national economy' – a term for economics now used in various languages. List criticized the classical school, in particular Smith, for holding a naïvely cosmopolitan view, in which nations are just associations of individuals that all benefit from peaceful division of labour and free trade. In reality, nations are the relevant subjects to be studied, since the productive forces of the association of industries at the national level are at least as strong as the effects of the division of labour. However, national industries benefit from free trade only at certain stages of development. At other stages nations can make progress only by making war or by protecting their emerging industries through tariffs or other restrictions.

Stage theories of economic development were no new concept; even Smith held a crude version. But it was List who popularized stage theories as a base for development policy. He argued that every nation, if it has the right resource potential, tends to pass through five stages, ranging from hunting and fishing to highly productive agriculture, manufacturing and commerce. His definition of development was 'progressive use of the productive forces'. List criticized the classical reduction of those forces to labour, land and capital, and included the social order, science and art, and the degree of liberty in the respective state.

At the highest stage of development, all nations would benefit from free trade. However, nations do not make progress simultaneously. There are leaders and followers, and the first part of List's book is about the historical succession of leading nations – from the Italian city republics of the Middle Ages to the United States of America as the prospective leader of the future. List described England as the leading nation of his time, flooding the rest of the world with her manufactured goods while retaining her own protection from imports (by 1841, the corn laws and other trade barriers were still in force). The small states in Germany used tariffs in trade with each other, but not in trade with England from where they wished to buy advanced products. In List's view, this hindered the release of productive forces in Germany. If the German states formed a customs union (*Zollverein*), abolishing internal tariffs while setting up a system of common external tariffs, their fledgling industries could make use of cost advantages in domestic trade. They would eventually reach the highest stage, at which they could compete with English manufacturers and Germany could also enjoy the benefits of free trade. List does not fit any pattern because he used classical, mercantilist and romantic concepts, while rejecting the core ideas of all these schools. His book was divided in an exemplary fashion into four parts – history, theory (his own), systems (the history of thought in critical perspective) and policy (trade strategies of different nations) – and yet he mixed these perspectives in all four parts. The essence of his long and winding argument was that the principle of free trade holds only at the primitive stages of economic development and when all nations have achieved the highest stage. Before that ideal end state, protectionism is required to make free trade feasible; it is the 'natural right of the late-comers'. As mentioned before, List's ideas have been a powerful influence in later developments of theories of development policy.

Historical schools

There are at least five historical schools in economic thinking: the English, the French, and the older, younger and youngest German schools. Apart from the younger German historical school none of them was really a school in the sense of holding a unified doctrine and professed membership, but they all have some ideas in common. These ideas were most clearly expressed in the works of the German historical schools, with which we begin.

The older historical school in Germany

The breakthrough of historicism in academic economics is connected with the names of Bruno Hildebrand (1812–78), Wilhelm Roscher (1817–94), and Karl Knies (1821–98) – three German university professors who are generally considered the founding fathers of the (older) historical school. Roscher's outline of economic lectures that he held at the University of Göttingen 'according to the historical method' (*Grundriß zu Vorlesungen über die Staatswirthschaft, Nach geschichtlicher Methode*, 1843) provided the starting point.

In the preface to the *Grundriß*, Roscher stated the four principles of the historical method that he was aiming to use in his lectures and in future research. First, he argued, the true aim of economic thinking is not to maximize the 'wealth of nations', but to understand the economic development of different nations; for this it is necessary to combine economic thinking with other disciplines, such as law, political science and arts. Second, a nation is not only made up of its 'presently living individuals', but also of its past, which must be studied in its different cultural stages. Third, the problem of identifying the essential regularities – so-called 'parallelisms' – in a great mass of phenomena calls for the use of a comparative empirical method. Fourth, the historical method does not permit the conclusion that observed institutions are good or bad as such, but it furthers the understanding of their functionality and eventual obsolescence by describing the contexts in which such institutions first emerge and later turn obsolete. Roscher explicitly set his method apart from that of Ricardo, even though he did not see it as 'opposed to the latter, since it gratefully makes use of the results' of Ricardian political economy.

While Roscher led the comparatively quiet life of a university professor, first at Göttingen, then at Leipzig, the lives of Hildebrand and Knies were more turbulent. They were both politically active prior to and after the democratic revolution of 1848, and both had to spend some time in Swiss exile before they were allowed to return to German academia. The political engagements of Hildebrand and Knies may explain why they stressed, even more than Roscher, the political and empirical aspects of economic reasoning.

In his book on economics in the present and the future (*National-Oekonomie der Gegenwart und Zukunft*, 1848), Hildebrand taught a stage theory of economic development that differed from earlier versions. According to Hildebrand, history should be understood as the transformation of primitive exchange economies into monetary economies and finally into credit economies. The latter are characterized by high productivity, mutual trust and social policies for the welfare of the workers. Knies wrote three large volumes about money and credit (*Das Geld*, 1873, *Der Credit*, I: 1876, II: 1879), but did not believe that credit economies could ever work without being based on gold or other metallic money reserves. In his early manifesto – *Die politische Ökonomie vom Standpunkte der geschichtlichen Methode*, 1853 – Knies had espoused the historical method even more fervently than Roscher and Hildebrand, emphasizing that political economy must describe the economic life of the people historically and analyse it on an ethical basis. Both Knies and Hildebrand were much in favour of empirical and in particular statistical work. They wrote about statistics as an independent and auxiliary science, and helped to set up statistical offices.

Two things are noteworthy about the relationship of the older historical school to classical and neoclassical economic thinking: the ambiguous attitude of Roscher, Hildebrand and Knies towards classical political economy, and their formative influence on Austrian neoclassical thinking. The three historicists presented their method as critique of the 'abstract' arguments and methods employed by Smith and Ricardo. But they had also much praise for the classical writers, and in most of their works they did not follow their own principles. They used classical methods and styles of arguments rather than the historical and interdisciplinary approach they had envisaged. Roscher and Knies developed notions of marginal utility and other concepts of subjectivist theories of value that can be dubbed 'proto-neoclassical', i.e. anticipating central elements of the 'marginalist revolution' (described in Chapter 4). At least two of the leading figures of Austrian neoclassicism, Böhm-Bawerk and Wieser, were in fact students of Knies at the University of Heidelberg. The older historical school thus paved the way for 'Austrian economics', whereas the younger historical school came into conflict with Austrian neoclassicists to the extent that the latter began to understand that they were a school of their own.

The younger historical school in Germany

It is not easy to determine which economists belong to the younger German historical school. The usual lists of names include, among others, the propagator of the 'state theory of money' Georg Friedrich Knapp (1842–1926), the social reformer Lujo Brentano (1844–1931), and the sociologist Werner Sombart (1863–1941) and Max Weber (1864–1920). Yet there is no doubt that the head of the younger historical school was Gustav von Schmoller (1838–1917), a prolific writer and editor of various journals and encyclopaedic works, who ruled the profession for many decades from his chair at the University of Berlin. Schmoller denied the existence of general economic laws more categorically than any other representative of the historical schools, arguing that economists could, at best, find some recurrent patterns in detailed historical investigations of economic phenomena, public administration and social policy in different epochs. Schmoller rejected not only the classical doctrines, but also the deterministic stage theories and 'impartial attitude' of the older historical school. He stressed that history holds lessons for present economic and social policy, but only if it is studied with a holistic approach that goes beyond isolating the economic logic of the course of events. As Schumpeter (1954, p. 812) has expressed it, 'the Schmollerian economist was in fact a historically minded sociologist in the latter term's widest meaning'.

In the person of Schmoller the German historical school overlapped with another prominent movement of the time, the so-called 'socialists of the chair' (*Kathedersozialisten*). These were no socialists in the generic sense of struggling for community control of production and income distribution; on the contrary, the socialists of the chair were mostly conservative professors and members of parliament who firmly opposed Marxism and other ideas of social revolution. Yet they also rejected the *laissez faire*-liberalism of the so-called Manchester school, which had popularized some of the doctrines of classical political economy in England, Germany and elsewhere. The socialists of the chair saw an urgent need for social policy in order to deal with the 'labour question', i.e. the social problems of poverty, unemployment and political unrest that arose in the industrialization process of their time.

The Berlin professor Adolph Wagner (1835–1917) was the most prominent *Kathedersozialist*. He recommended an extensive and systematic combination of economic and social policy, unlike Schmoller who suggested selective measures and pragmatism. Disregarding Schmoller's general rejection of economic laws, Wagner formulated his famous 'law of increasing public expenditure' from observations of a tendency of public spending to grow as a share of the gross domestic product. Wagner's law pertains to government intervention in three areas: to increased spending on health insurance, pension schemes and other instruments of social policy, to an expansion of activities in monetary and fiscal policy, and to an increase in public ownership of all types of assets.

To promote their ideas efficiently, members of the historical school and related circles founded the *Verein für Socialpolitik* in 1873. This association held (and still holds) regular meetings of academic economists, practitioners and politicians, and it has produced a large number of series of publications in many subfields of economics. It came to serve as a model for economist associations in other countries, in particular for the *American Economic Association* (see below).

The German historical schools set their focus on methodological problems of economic thinking, and the *Verein für Socialpolitik* was the forum of two great battles over methods and norms, the *Methodenstreit* and the *Werturteilsstreit*. If neither the German historicists nor the Austrian neoclassicists defined themselves as schools before the 1880s, they definitely started to do just that in the course of the *Methodenstreit*. This battle over methods started when Menger published his investigation of the methods of social science (*Untersuchungen über die Methode der Socialwissenschaften und der politischen Oekonomie insbesondere*) in 1883. Menger stressed the primacy of theoretical analysis over historical research, which in his view only has an auxiliary function. Schmoller reacted by asserting that it was obvious that the inductive method of the historical school, based on meticulous studies of facts, was far superior to the sterile deductivism of the obsolete traditions that Menger represented. Menger retorted with an utterly polemical pamphlet on the 'the errors of historicism' (1884). Thereafter the two adversaries remained silent, but the battle over inductivism versus deductivism in economic thinking raged on for decades, carried out by numerous epigones. Even so, the frontlines were not always clear. Wagner, for example, sided with Menger in the *Methodenstreit*, even though he was in all other respects in Schmoller's camp.

The second round of controversies, the *Werturteilsstreit* (battle over norms), started at the 1909 meetings of the *Verein*. The adversaries were the younger historical school under Schmoller and the circles of Sombart and Weber, which Schumpeter (1954, pp. 815–20) dubbed 'the "youngest" historical school' (Schumpeter himself can be considered a member of that school; his monumental *History of Economic Analysis*, posthumously published in 1954, was based on his 1914 contribution to Weber's encyclopaedic *Grundriss der Sozialökonomik*). Sombart and Weber, professors at Berlin and Heidelberg, protested against the confusion of description and value judgments that permeated the works of the younger historical school. Weber argued that political or ethical norms cannot be derived from scientific observation and should therefore be strictly kept apart from all scientific work. Schmoller, on the other hand, considered 'national economy' to be a 'moral–political science' that is inevitably based on the norms of the elites of the respective nation and era.

The battles over methods and norms ended inconclusively. With hindsight much of the disagreement seemed to be a matter of emphasis rather than substance. Yet the core issues – the relation between inductive and deductive cognition, and the role of norms – have led to further controversies in other countries and disciplines, such as sociology and philosophy.

Other traditions of historicism

The historicist tradition in economic thinking was certainly strongest in Germany, but it was not confined to that country. An *English* or *British historical school* is frequently mentioned in the literature, but it comprises persons and ideas that had apparently little to do with each other, ranging from the Anglican cleric Richard Jones (1790–1855) to the 'pioneer of the British welfare state' Lord William Beveridge (1879–1963). The school label is a retrospective construction, using German historicism as its benchmark and picking British writers who in the same era held inductivist, historicist or reformist positions. Here we present only John Stuart Mill (1806–73), Walter Bagehot (1826–77), Beatrice Potter Webb (1858–1943) and her husband Sidney Webb (1859–1947).

Mill was an important classical thinker (see Chapter 3). However, towards the end of his life, he was increasingly in sympathy with the inductive approach to economic research. His views on social policy were close to those of the German socialists of the chair.

Bagehot was a journalist and early editor of *The Economist*, now a worldwide leading journal. *The Economist* was closely affiliated with the Manchester school, firmly propagating the principle of free trade and other classical doctrines. Yet Bagehot found the classical theories and policy prescriptions lacking historical and institutional content. In his *Lombard Street: A Description of the Money Market* (1873), he discussed the development of the English monetary system, with special regard to banking failures in financial crises. Bagehot became famous for urging the Bank of England to assume political responsibility as a *lender of last resort*, now a key principle of central banking.

The Webbs were the founders of the Fabian Society, a socialist movement that aimed at establishing a welfare state by redistributing rents to various ends of social policy. The Webbs had a mixed background in the writings of Ricardo, Marx, Marshall and the German historical school. They published numerous studies on industrial organization, poverty, trade unions and other labour-market aspects of British society, some together with Lord Beveridge. The Webbs are also noteworthy for founding the London School of Economics and Political Science (LSE) in 1895, an important institution of economic education and research.

In the case of France, it is more justified to speak of a historical school. Pierre Émile Levasseur (1828–1911) was the leader of the French historical school, but Clement Juglar (1819–1905), Charles Gide (1847–1932), Albert Aftalion (1874–1956) are more famous. The doctor and statistician Juglar was one of the first who, upon studying time series and other historical material in the 1850s and 1860s, discovered the empirical regularity of business cycles. The medium-term cycles with a frequency of seven to eleven years have been named after him. Aftalion followed in Juglar's footsteps and published on overinvestment theories of the business cycle in the early twentieth century. He was one of the first to formulate the *accelerator principle*, according to which aggregate investment reacts overproportionally to changes in aggregate consumption. Gide was an influential journal editor and historian of economic thought. He had strong leanings towards the German historical schools, but was also one of the few who supported Walras' theoretical work, since both were strongly interested in the co-operative movement of producers and consumers.

Institutionalism

The American institutionalist school was strongly influenced by the German historical schools. Two of its founding fathers, Richard T. Ely (1854–1943) and Edwin R.A. Seligman (1861–1939), had studied under Knies in Heidelberg. Even the neoclassicist John Bates Clark (see Chapter 4) had spent his formative years there, before he became the teacher of Thorstein Veblen (1857–1929), the most illustrious institutionalist. Using the German *Verein für Socialpolitik* as a model, Ely and others founded the American Economic Association (AEA) in 1885. (With its annual meetings and the *American*

Economic Review (AER), the *Journal of Economic Literature* (JEL), the *Journal of Economic Perspectives* (JEP) and four journals covering special areas of economics, the AEA is now the world's most influential society of economists.) The American institutionalists, too, went through several battles of methods. They dominated many economic departments at US universities in the early twentieth century, before they were gradually crowded out by neoclassical and Keynesian economists in the 1930s and 1940s.

American institutionalism (and traditional institutionalism in general) was based on the critique of the neoclassical reduction of institutions to products of rational behaviour determined by consumer preferences and technology. The institutionalists attempted, instead, to explain how tastes, technology and economic behaviour are shaped by institutions, which they defined widely as a system of 'habits of thought', rules and organizations that constitute the 'social order'. Consequently, they were interested in understanding the evolution of institutions as systems of social control of the economy.

Thorstein Veblen

Veblen is best known for his *Theory of the Leisure Class* (1899), one of the few economic classics that is recommended for leisure-time reading because of its satirical qualities. Veblen was born in Wisconsin; his parents were farmers who had emigrated from Norway. After extended studies at various American universities and self-study while recovering from malaria, he became professor of political economy at the newly founded University of Chicago in 1892. There he also served as editor for the *Journal of Political Economy* for ten years. In 1906, he had to leave Chicago because of his unconventional lifestyle, which allegedly included 'womanizing'. Veblen moved to Stanford University, from where he was dismissed in 1909, again because of extramarital affairs. His further stations were the University of Missouri, the US Food Administration in Washington, the newly founded New School of Social Research in New York, and finally a cottage near Stanford where he died in 1929.

In his *Theory of the Leisure Class* and even more so in his *Theory of Business Enterprise* (1904), Veblen described economic life as a process of ongoing evolution. Drawing on anthropological and psychological readings, he saw evolution as driven by conflicts of 'instincts', in particular workmanship, parental bent, idle curiosity on the one hand, and emulation and predation on the other. Workmanship and curiosity produce technical progress, whose potential for the economic and social improvement is not fully realized because of the 'archaic traits of emulation, domination and animism'. Institutions are the result of the interaction of technical progress with predation, the defence of vested interests and status thinking, expressed in the 'habits' of 'pecuniary emulation', 'conspicuous consumption' and 'conspicuous leisure'.

For Veblen, like Marx, history is shaped by class struggle, though not in battles over the means of production, but as a permanent conflict between the leisure class and the working class. According to Veblen's class concept, the leisure class comprises all those who are exempt from productive work – including the businessmen, as they do 'not really' produce goods, but simply shift them around. Engineers and (most) scientists are, on the other hand, considered to be part of the working class. Veblen's class concept is reminiscent of distinctions between productive and unproductive labour in physiocratic and classical writings.

Veblen's analysis of institutions was by no means apologetic. He did not, as is quite usual in current economics, praise existing institutions as functional responses to problems arising in the evolutionary process. On the contrary, Veblen had a rather pessimistic outlook on the progress of mankind:

> [T]he leisure class, in the nature of things, consistently acts to retard that adjustment to the environment which is called social advance or development. The characteristic attitude of the class may be summed up in the maxim: 'Whatever is, is right'; whereas the law of natural selection, as applied to human institutions, gives the axiom: 'Whatever is, is wrong.' Not that the institutions of to-day are wholly wrong for the purposes of the life to-day, but they are, always and in the nature of things, wrong to some extent. They are the result of a more or less inadequate adjustment of the methods of living to a situation which prevailed at some point in the past development . . . 'Right' and 'wrong' are of course here used without conveying any reflection as to what ought or ought not to be. They are simply applied from the (morally colourless) evolutionary standpoint, and are intended to designate compatibility or incompatibility with the effective evolutionary process.
>
> (Veblen 1979 [1899], pp. 206–7)

Other institutionalists

The Wisconsin professor John R. Commons (1862–1945) was one of the early institutionalists who systematically discussed the tasks of institutional economics, in particular in relationship with the making and interpretation of law. In an influential AER article of 1931 he defined the subject in the general terms of 'collective action':

An institution is defined as collective action in control, liberation and expansion of individual action. Its forms are unorganized custom and organized going concerns. The individual action is participation in bargaining, managing and rationing transactions, which are the ultimate units of economic activity. The control by custom or concerns consists in working rules which govern more or less what the individual can, must, or may do or not do . . . Transactions determine legal control, while the classical and hedonic economics was concerned with physical control. Legal control is future physical control.

(Commons 1931, p. 648)

Institutional economics is about legal control, and hence about 'future physical control'. It has thus a wider scope of analysis than classical or 'hedonic' (alias neoclassical) economics.

Another influential American institutionalist was Wesley C. Mitchell (1874–1948), who was a student of Veblen at Chicago and later economics professor at Columbia University in New York. Mitchell is renowned for setting up and directing the National Bureau of Economic Research, an important think-tank, and for his empirical work on business cycles, which, however, has been attacked as 'measurement without theory'.

In the context of American institutionalists we may also mention Allyn A. Young (1876–1929) and Frank H. Knight (1885–1972), who combined elements of neoclassical and institutional economics. Young's research on the role of increasing returns to scale in the growth process of an economy has paved the way for modern growth theory. Knight's *Risk, Uncertainty and Profit* (1921) was a key contribution to modern decision theory. It introduced the distinction between probabilistic risk, which can be handled by insurance, and uncertainty, whose acceptance requires 'entrepreneurial spirit'.

Two other North American economists who combined institutionalism with other approaches were John Kenneth Galbraith (1908–2006) and Kenneth Ewart Boulding (1910–93). Galbraith's writings contain elements of both institutionalism and Keynesianism (see Chapter 6). With about 30 books, written in a literary style and challenging mainstream economics and conventional wisdom, he was one of the most well-known economists among the general public in the first decades after the Second World War. In *The Affluent Society* (1958) Galbraith maintains that there is a tendency in a capitalist market economy to overproduce private consumer goods while the public sector is undersupported. In *The New Industrial State* (1967) he emphasizes the governing role of modern large corporations and the power of technical experts in those corporations. Boulding was a broad social scientist and one of the protagonists of evolutionary economics. He urged an integration of economics with biological concepts of ecological equilibrium and dynamics and genetic production (see also Chapter 7).

What remains of historicism and institutionalism?

The immediate answer is: histories and institutions. Members of the schools described in this chapter made valuable contributions to the writing of economic history, and some of them – for example, Gide, Knight and Schumpeter – were notable historians of economic thought. As pointed out above, many of the important institutions in current economics – schools and research institutes, associations and journals – were founded by members of the historical and institutionalist schools. Even so, economists nowadays often consider those schools as outdated and atheoretical (if they know them at all). Yet historicism and institutionalism have set various impulses for further progress in economic thinking, partly in critique, but partly also in extension of neoclassical economics. We will discuss some of that progress in Chapter 7.

Summing up, we should take note of two other remarkable results of nineteenth- and twentieth-century historicism and institutionalism. The first is the development of development economics, which owes much to ideas inherited from these schools. It is no coincidence that those schools developed most strongly in Germany and the United States. Both were, compared to Britain and France, latecomers to economic development. Attempting to catch up with the leading nations, economists in both countries had a keener eye for the development of institutions that foster development, including protectionist trade policies. As there are still latecomers in economic development and eras of great transformation (for example, Eastern Europe and China since the 1990s), the relativist approaches keep enjoying some popularity.

The second result is a differentiation of disciplines, ironically arising from the holistic view of economic, cultural and other social phenomena. The development of economic history as a separate subdiscipline was clearly an outgrowth of the work of the historical schools. Moreover, much of the development of sociology as an independent science can be ascribed to works and initiatives of historicists and institutionalists. Several disciplines today lay claim to some of the representatives of those schools, while others are hardly accepted by any discipline. For example, Weber, Veblen and Sombart are ranked among the pioneers of sociology. Likewise, the Swedish economist and Nobel prize winner Gunnar Myrdal (1898–1987), who described himself sometimes as a 'late institutionalist', is often regarded as a sociologist. We will take a look at Myrdal's macroeconomic contribution in the next chapter, and end this chapter with his solomonic suggestion for solving the *Werturteilsstreit*.

As a young professor at Stockholm University in the late 1920s, Myrdal firmly advocated the Weberian imperative of keeping research free from value judgments. Later on in life – after further experience in social research and politics – Myrdal came to the conclusion that it is impossible to do research without prior value judgments. In his *Objectivity in Social Research* (1969), Myrdal argued:

> [B]iases in social science cannot be erased simply by 'keeping to the facts' and refining the methods of dealing with statistical data. Indeed, data and the handling of data are often more susceptible to tendencies towards bias than is 'pure thought'. The chaos of possible data for research does not organize itself into systematic knowledge by mere observation. . . . If, in their attempts to be factual, scientists do not make their viewpoint explicit, they leave room for biases.
>
> (Myrdal 1969, p. 51)

Myrdal's solution to the *Werturteilsstreit* – researchers should always make their norms explicit – is simple in principle, but apparently difficult to practise.

References

Commons, John R. (1931) Institutional Economics, *American Economic Review* 21: 648–57.

Galbraith, John Kenneth (1958) *The Affluent Society*. Boston, MA: Houghton Mifflin.

Galbraith, John Kenneth (1967) *The New Industrial State*. Princeton, NJ: Princeton University Press.

List, Friedrich (1885) [1841] *The National System of Political Economy*, translation Sampson S. Lloyd. London: Longmans, Green, and Co.

Myrdal, Gunnar (1969) *Objectivity in Social Research*. New York: Pantheon.

Roscher, Wilhelm (1843) *Grundriß zu Vorlesungen über die Staatswirthschaft, Nach der geschichtlichen Methode*. Göttingen: Dieterichsche Buchhandlung.

Schumpeter, Joseph A. (1954) *History of Economic Analysis*. Oxford: Oxford University Press. Part IV.

Sowell, Thomas (1987) Veblen, Thorstein. *The New Palgrave: A Dictionary of Economics*. London: Macmillan.

Streissler, Erich (1990) The Influence of German Economics on the Work of Menger and Marshall, in Bruce J. Caldwell (ed.), *Carl Menger and His Legacy in Economics*. London: Duke University Press.

Trautwein, Hans-Michael (2002) The Credit Theory of Carl Knies, in Stephan Boehm, Christian Gehrke, Heinz D. Kurz and Richard Sturn (eds), *Is There Progress in Economics?* Cheltenham: Edward Elgar.

Trautwein, Hans-Michael (2003) G.F. Knapp: An Economist with Institutional Complexion, in Warren Samuels (ed.), *European Economists of the Early 20th Century*, vol. 2. Cheltenham, Northampton: Edward Elgar.

Veblen, Thorstein (1979) [1899] *The Theory of the Leisure Class*. New York: Penguin Books.

6 Monetary macroeconomics

In its analysis of price formation in market economies, neoclassical economics has evolved around a dichotomy (bipartition of theory), that is at the centre of a perennial debate about money. In the microeconomic reasoning that is based on the individual decisions of consumers and producers, the *structure* of prices is determined by the marginal principle (see Chapter 4). In the macroeconomic determination of aggregate production, some version of the time-honoured quantity theory of money is usually invoked to explain any change in the general *level* of prices as the result of changes in the volume of money in the same direction (see Chapter 2). This analytical separation between money prices and relative prices implies that money is neutral with regard to real economic activity: An increase (decrease) in the volume of money could make the total demand for goods and services exceed (fall short of) supply, thereby causing the price level to rise (fall). But such monetary impulses cannot change the allocation of resources to the extent that the structure and level of real output and income will be affected, at least not in the long run. Monetary changes may temporarily disturb the price mechanism that equilibrates aggregate supply and demand, but they cannot permanently keep it out of order. Sooner or later, the price mechanism will return the market system to its *initial* equilibrium position in real terms. Or so it was believed in the first decades after the 'marginalist revolution'. There was no theory that would make a rigorous connection of the marginal principle with the quantity theory.

In the 1920s and 1930s, the period between the First and Second World Wars, the gap between 'pure price theory' and monetary theory came to be seen as a serious challenge to neoclassical theory and its claim to general validity. The dichotomy made it difficult to analyse the observable links between the extreme booms and depressions, and the monetary disorder of the time, which included severe deflation and hyperinflation. The microeconomic approach of neoclassical economics was clearly in need of macrotheoretical foundations, if not fundamental alterations. The struggle to overcome this dichotomy was the starting point for the development of modern monetary macroeconomics which has revolved around the issue of the (long-run) neutrality of money ever since. It has mostly done so in the dialectical motion of thesis, antithesis and synthesis. Many textbooks describe this in terms of controversies between neoclassical and Keynesian macroeconomics (or supply-side and demand-side economics), now allegedly dissolved into a 'synthetic' consensus view. We find it more useful to organize the discussion of the history of macroeconomics along its connections with the monetary theories of Wicksell and Fisher.

Wicksell and Fisher Connections

By and large, monetary economics has developed along two different lines (see Figure 7). The first line has been labelled the *Wicksell Connection* (Leijonhufvud 1981), since it can be traced back to Knut Wicksell's theory of cumulative processes of inflation that arise from failures of the market rate of interest to coordinate planned aggregate investment and saving. The second line of argument can be labelled the *Fisher Connection*, since it is based on Irving Fisher's reformulation of the quantity theory of money and his views on the determination of interest rates and intertemporal equilibrium.

Wicksell's monetary theory

Wicksell's contributions to capital theory and public finance have been outlined in Chapter 4. Another important contribution is his *Geldzins und Güterpreise* (1898), a treatise about interest rates and changes in the price level. Wicksell's ambition was to reformulate the quantity theory of money for an economy in which the volume of money is no longer given by gold findings or other accidental circumstances, but determined by the market interaction of prices for goods and capital. He pointed out that, in modern financial systems, most payments are made by transfers between bank accounts. Many of these accounts are created when banks extend loans to their borrowers and grant them the corresponding amounts in terms of deposits. In the flows of expenditure and income they are transferred to sellers of goods and labour who in turn partly hold them as savings. The banks use these saving funds as reserves for extending additional loans to finance the production of goods. They are thus key players in the capital market, coordinating the aggregate saving and investment in the economy and creating additional money in response to demands for finance of 'real investment'. Whether such additional demands arise depends on the relationship between the 'costs of capital' in terms of the banks' lending rate – in Wicksell's terminology the 'money rate' or '*market rate of interest*' – and

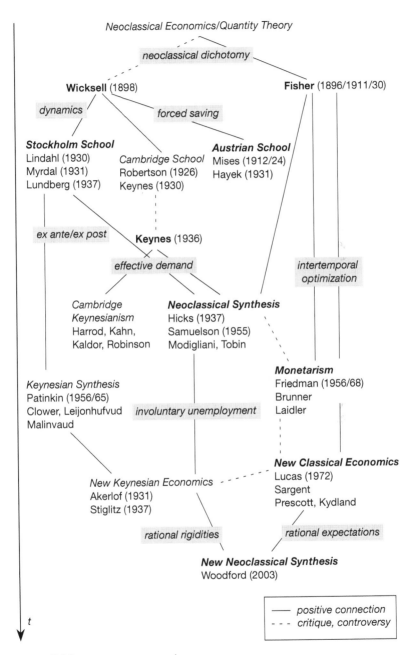

Figure 7 Monetary macroeconomics

the rate of return to the capital invested in goods production. Wicksell called the rate of return, at which, in the aggregate, planned real investment equals planned saving, the *'natural rate of interest'*.

According to Wicksell, inflation develops if the natural rate exceeds the market rate of interest (for example, due to some innovations in technology), giving rise to profit expectations that raise the demand for loans and investment goods. Since banks tend to accommodate credit demand at the going rate of interest (as they earn their profits on fees and spreads between deposit and lending rates), the credit expansion will produce an increase in nominal income and aggregate demand beyond full capacity supply. Sooner or later, prices will rise in a cumulative fashion. The process of inflation will continue as long as the market rate falls short of the capital rate of interest. When the two rates happen to coincide again, the price level in the new equilibrium will be higher than the price level at the outset of the *cumulative process*.

Interest rates are relative prices, since they induce an intertemporal exchange, between monetary claims on goods now and on goods in the future. By making a connection between interest rates and changes in 'absolute' money prices, Wicksell overcame the neoclassical dichotomy in the determination of the structure and level of prices. By making specific assumptions that largely excluded significant real effects of cumulative inflation or deflation, however, Wicksell claimed, but did not show, that money is neutral. In that respect, Wicksell retained the neoclassical dichotomy.

Fisher's monetary theory

Fisher's contributions to capital theory have been described in Chapter 4. Like Wicksell, he also was a monetary theorist. His most famous work is *The Purchasing Power of Money* (1911), in which he formulated the quantity theory in terms of the *equation of exchange, $MV = PT$*, where M denotes the volume of money, V its velocity of circulation, P the level of prices, and T the 'real' volume of transactions in the relevant period (T can under certain assumptions also be replaced by Y, the national real income). This equation is basically an identity, but is normally interpreted as a functional relationship, in which the price level is causally and proportionally determined by the volume of money (V and T are considered as independent variables that are constant, at least in the short run).

Another element of Fisher's monetary theory is his distinction between nominal and real interest rates. Already in his *Appreciation and Interest* (1896), Fisher argued that inflation causes nominal rates of interest to change proportionally, at least in the long run. In terms of this *Fisher effect*, the real rate of interest can be approximated by the difference between the (level of the) nominal rate and the rate of inflation (as long as the latter is not high). This relationship, too, is an identity, but serves as a condition for equilibrium in financial markets, if inflation is understood as 'expected inflation'. The underlying rationale is that financial investors will not provide loans unless they can protect their real income by adjusting interest rates to changes in inflation.

The Fisher effect is based on the hypothesis that the real rate of interest is independent of changes in the monetary sphere. In Fisher's view it is essentially determined by the *intertemporal optimization* of consumption and leisure, as the relative price of consumption now and consumption in the future. Yet Fisher did not systematically connect this 'real side' of his theory of interest with his quantity-theoretical explanation of inflation. In this way he retained the neoclassical dichotomy, merely postulating the neutrality of money.

Connections

At first sight, there do not seem to be great differences between the views of Wicksell and Fisher. Both of them defended the quantity theory and postulated the long-run neutrality of money. Both nevertheless propagated an active policy of price-level stabilization that helps to avoid social conflicts which could develop if inflation or deflation lead to the redistribution of real incomes. Yet further extensions of Wicksell's approach to the theory of interest took critical turns against the neutrality doctrine. Relaxing some of Wicksell's restrictive assumptions, his followers in the Austrian, Stockholm and Keynesian schools opened various avenues to the analysis of the interaction between the market rate of interest and changes in *relative* prices, employment and real national income. Fisher's contributions, dichotomically separated in his own writings, were recombined by his monetarist and new classical followers, so as to overcome the dichotomy and yet arrive at the result of the neutrality of money.

In the following we describe as a *Fisher Connection* a tradition of macroeconomic theories in which the economy is continuously in intertemporal equilibrium, with the interest rate just measuring society's discount of the future, and in which money is neutral. The *Wicksell Connection*, on the other hand, represents theories in which the market rate of interest can fail to keep the economy in intertemporal equilibrium, and in which monetary variables can affect real economic activity. For the sake of fairness, it should be noted that Fisher himself did not consider money to be neutral in the short run, and that he developed a debt-deflation theory that casts doubt on the long-run neutrality of money. However, he did this only in 1933, with specific reference to the Great Depression, and without systematic connection with the rest of his work. At the time, some writers in the Wicksell Connection had already begun to make progress in transforming the existing plethora of conjectures about business cycles into more rigorous structures of macro-economic theory.

Business cycles and macrodynamics

The term *macroeconomics* was only coined in the mid-1930s, apparently by the Norwegian economist Ragnar Frisch (1895–1973), one of the pioneers of econometrics and first Nobel prize winners. Until then, the analysis of changes in total output, the price level and other aggregate variables was largely considered to be the domain of business cycle theory. There was an enormous variety of approaches to explain cyclical fluctuations of economic activity, with equally many and mostly incompatible policy conclusions. During the Great Depression, the League of Nations (the predecessor of the United Nations) ran a project on 'the causes and cures of depressions', in which they commissioned a systematic analysis and synthesis of business cycle theories in search for viable strategies of economic stabilization. The outcome was the excellent survey *Prosperity and Depression* (1937) by Gottfried Haberler (1900–95), an Austrian economist who later became a Harvard professor. In the survey, the existing approaches were grouped into 'purely monetary', 'overinvestment', 'maladjustment', 'underconsumption', 'psychological' and 'harvest theories' of the business cycle. In the synthetical part, the importance of the acceleration principle was stressed (see Chapter 5), and cyclical upswings and downswings were described in terms of cumulative processes.

While Haberler's book was on the reading lists of courses in business-cycle theory for more than half a century, his synthesis hardly ever made an impact on the design of stabilization policy. The latter was more strongly influenced by macroeconomics, which began to develop as a separate field in the 1930s. It had its own synthesis in the IS-LM model, which still survives in many macroeconomic textbooks. It, too, can be traced back to 1937, to a paper by the Oxford economist John R. Hicks (1904–89) on *Mr Keynes and the Classics*. Before we come to Keynes, Hicks and the IS-LM model, we will take a look at the split between business cycle theory and macroeconomics in the Wicksell Connection, exemplified by the Austrian school and the Stockholm school.

Austrian business cycle theory

Wicksell had meant his *Interest and Prices* to provide a theory of (secular) inflation and deflation, but not of the business cycle. He regarded the cycle as an entirely 'real' phenomenon, caused by disturbances of the economy through irregular technical progress. Friedrich August von Hayek (1899–1992), a second-generation member of the Austrian school of neoclassical economics, nevertheless came to use Wicksell's approach in order to satisfy two purposes at once. The first purpose was to provide a general explanation of the business cycle; the second was to integrate monetary theory with neoclassical general equilibrium theory, i.e. to overcome the dichotomy.

Hayek's Austrian business cycle theory, also known as ABC theory, is based on an idea of Ludwig von Mises (1881–1973), another second-generation Austrian. Hayek expounded it in 1931, in four lectures on *Prices and Production* given at the London School of Economics, where he moved from Vienna in the same year. Hayek argued that misguided monetary policy can make the market rate of interest stay below the equilibrium rate (Wicksell's 'natural rate'). The gap leads to a credit boom and a monetary expansion that redistributes purchasing power to the borrowing firms. Their demands for investment goods necessarily change the *structures* of prices and production and force households to abstain from consumption due to rising prices (forced saving). According to Hayek, the expansion must, however, inevitably find its end in a crisis. Sooner or later consumption goods become so scarce that the structure of prices and production is reversed, making many half-completed investment projects unfeasible. The crisis will return the system to its original level of planned saving and investment, as determined by general equilibrium theory.

Hayek's beliefs that the crisis is a cure and that monetary policy should be restrictive and neutral did not make his ABC theory very popular in the middle of the Great Depression. It was also criticized as logically unfounded by Sraffa and other economists at the time. In recent decades, the ABC theory has nevertheless made an occasional comeback whenever monetary expansion has ended in a financial crisis with a large number of failed long-term projects.

The Stockholm school

In 1936, John Maynard Keynes of Cambridge University, one of the leading economists of the time, published his *General Theory of Employment, Interest and Money*. The book immediately attracted great attention, not least because its famous author had announced that it would revolutionize economics. A year later, Bertil Ohlin (whom we have met in the context of trade theory in Chapter 3) claimed in two long articles in the *Economic Journal* (which was edited by Keynes) that a group of Swedish economists had anticipated and, in some aspects, advanced beyond Keynes's *General Theory*. The group included Erik Lindahl (1891–1960), Gunnar Myrdal (1898–1987) and Ohlin (1899–1979) himself in the older generation, and Erik Lundberg (1907–87) plus a few others in the younger. Ohlin gave the group its name, the *Stockholm school*, even though not all of its members worked in the Swedish capital. Moreover, most of them stressed the differences between their theories and policy views much more than the similarities. They nevertheless shared a common outlook and some of their contributions merit a brief summary.

The first highlights in the macroeconomics of the Stockholm school were set by Lindahl's *Penningpolitikens medel* (1930, translated as *Part II: The Rate of Interest and the Price Level*, 1939) and Myrdal's *Om penningteoretisk jämvikt* (1931, *Monetary Equilibrium*, 1939). In critical examination of Wicksell's *Interest and Prices*, both authors argued that the quantity theory and the static equilibrium analysis of neoclassical price theory are unsuitable for dealing with changes in the price level, output and the distribution of income. They, like many other members of the Stockholm school, stressed the need to develop a dynamic macroeconomic theory, in which the formation of expectations is a central issue. On the one hand, firms and producers base their plans for transactions on their expectations of prices, quantities and other outcomes of the market process. On the other hand, those outcomes often differ from the agents' original plans, so that expectations are not fulfilled and hence might have to be adjusted in the following periods. Such adjustment processes can take the character of cumulative processes of inflation and deflation, in which – depending on initial conditions and other factors – output may change and unemployment emerge. Myrdal coined the terms *ex ante* and *ex post* in order to distinguish between planned values and effective values of the relevant variables. The *ex ante/ex post* terminology and the scenario technique, i.e. the distinction between different sequences of plans and adjustments, have been lasting contributions of the Stockholm school to macroeconomic thinking.

The most systematic efforts to develop a macrodynamic theory along these lines were made by Lindahl and Lundberg. Lindahl (1939) laid out the framework for a sequence analysis of price formation in disequilibrium. He assumed that sellers set prices according to their expectations which frequently turn out to be false (*ex post*). Selling at 'false prices' in some markets create excess supplies and demands that feed through to the whole system of markets and lead to adjustments of expectations and prices in further transactions. Yet, in Lindahl's view, market processes are driven by expectations without any inherent tendency towards general equilibrium. His sequence analysis anticipated the Keynesian theories that in the 1970s came to emphasize the role of false prices for the determination of effective demand.

However, Lindahl also anticipated elements of monetarism, demanding that monetary policy should aim strictly at stabilizing the price level in order to stabilize the formation of expectations in the market process. He suggested that the central bank should be given full instrumental independence from other authorities, an idea that gained prominence and was realized in various parts of the world towards the end of the twentieth century.

Lundberg's *Studies in the Theory of Economic Expansion* (1937) is another example of early dynamic macroeconomics. It is one of the first publications where we find elements of modern growth theory in exact definitions of the conditions for steady-state growth. Lundberg uses them as a benchmark for the analysis of model sequences that include crisis scenarios with Hayekian overinvestment and Keynesian undersaving, reduced to their common Wicksellian core.

Keynes and the Keynesians

The *General Theory of Employment, Interest and Money* (1936) made an impact on economic thinking – precisely as its author Keynes had expected. The book is often seen as the beginning of a revolution in macroeconomic policy, even though it is disputed in how far there really was a change in substance of theorizing and policymaking (see Laidler 1999). The *General Theory* was widely read and respected as the bible of macroeconomics – though perhaps not exactly in the way its author had expected. It is difficult to say what Keynes would have thought about all the interpretations of his *General Theory* which have come to circulate among economists. Here we will have to make do with a short account of the ideas that Keynes himself considered to be central and what survived of them in different Keynesianisms.

John Maynard Keynes

The son of John Neville Keynes, a well-known economics lecturer at Cambridge University, John Maynard Keynes (1883–1946) came to be the most eminent among the Cambridge economists. He studied economics under Marshall and Pigou. During the First World War, Keynes worked for the British treasury, which he represented at the Versailles peace conference in 1919. He earned worldwide fame for *The Economic Consequences of the Peace* (1919), a critical examination of the harsh obligations that the Versailles treaty had forced upon Germany. Keynes returned to academic life at Cambridge, edited the *Economic Journal* (he was its editor from 1911 until 1945), made a fortune on financial speculation, managed the funds of King's College, and founded the British Arts Council. During the Second World War Keynes was again involved in political missions, most importantly in the negotiations preceding the Bretton Woods agreement on international monetary cooperation. Keynes proposed to establish a supranational central bank and the Bancor, a synthetic unit of account for the clearing of balances of payment. Due to the bargaining power of the US government the negotiations led to less radical arrangements, but various elements of later initiatives towards monetary integration – including the creation of the ECU and the Euro – can be traced back to the Keynes Plan for the post-war monetary order.

Keynes wrote a number of books, of which we single out only two. The first is his *Treatise on Money* (1930), a work in two volumes that puts him firmly in the Wicksell Connection as it explains credit cycles in terms of the interaction of interest-rate gaps with fluctuations in the price level. In the following years, during the Great Depression, Keynes shifted his focus from cumulative price changes to cumulative changes in real output and income. The result was his *General Theory of Employment, Interest and Money* (1936). In the preface to the French edition, Keynes summarized his key points:

> I have called my theory a *general* theory. I mean by this that I am chiefly concerned with the behaviour of the economic system as a whole . . . It is shown that, generally speaking, the actual level of output and employ-ment depends, not on the capacity to produce or on the pre-existing level of incomes, but on the current decisions to produce which depend in turn on current decisions to invest and on present expectations of current and prospective consumption.
>
> (Keynes 1973, pp. xxxii–iii)

Keynes thus emphasized that the levels of production and employment are determined by the *principle of effective demand*, and not by supply of capital and labour, as postulated by Say's law (see Chapter 2). Furthermore, the interest rate assumes a role quite different from the task of coordinating saving and investment which had been assigned to it by neoclassical economics.

> It is the function of the rate of interest to preserve equilibrium, not between the demand and the supply of new capital goods, but between the demand and the supply of money, that is to say between the demand for *liquidity* and the means of satisfying this demand.
>
> (Keynes 1973, p. xxxiv)

The rate of interest is thus determined by *liquidity preference*. It is defined as a sort of risk premium for those who abstain from holding their wealth in its most liquid form, which is money. It determines both the levels of real income and prices and, hence, refutes the neoclassical dichotomy:

I have called this book the *General Theory of Employment, Interest and Money*; and the third feature to which I may call attention is the treatment of money and prices. The following analysis registers my final escape from the confusions of the Quantity Theory, which once entangled me. I regard the price level as a whole as being determined in precisely the same way as individual prices; that is to say, under the influence of supply and demand . . . The quantity of money determines the supply of liquid resources, and hence the rate of interest, and in conjunction with other factors (particularly that of confidence) the inducement to invest, which in turn fixes the equilibrium level of incomes, output and employment and (at each stage in conjunction with other factors) the price-level as a whole through the influences of supply and demand thus established.

(Keynes 1973, pp. xxxiv–v)

The key ideas in Keynes's *General Theory* are thus found in the combination of the principle of effective demand, liquidity preference, and the *marginal efficiency of capital*, the internal rate of return on marginal real investment.

Keynes assumed that supply adjusts to demand within a short time. Therefore he could keep his theory in the simple terms of *comparative-static equilibrium analysis*. In his view, total demand was more important for employment than the structural details of supply-side adjustments. Hence he could keep his analysis on an *aggregate* level. Macroeconomic equilibrium was defined as the combination of aggregate real income and the market rate of interest at which total demand in goods markets and financial markets equals supply. This definition implies the working of a mechanism of quantity adjustments by which aggregate income is transformed into expenditures such that saving will equal investment. Contrary to the logic of neoclassical economics, investment is, in Keynes's view, not determined by saving and the marginal productivity of capital that in equilibrium equals the rate of interest. It is the other way round: changes in investment are caused by changes in the market rate of interest and the marginal efficiency of capital, and they induce the changes in aggregate income that produce the saving required to equal investment *ex post*.

Keynes thus postulated an income mechanism that resembled some of the sequences in the models of the Stockholm school, but he put stronger emphasis on their characterization as self-contained quantity adjustments rather than intermediate phases of price adjustments. The income mechanism was, moreover, distinguished from the Wicksellian interest-rate mechanism that Keynes had put to the foreground in his *Treatise on Money* (1930). (This is why, in Figure 7, the connection between Keynes 1930 and 1936 is a broken line.)

According to Keynes, and contrary to the neoclassical interpretation of Say's law, macroeconomic equilibrium is compatible with *involuntary unemployment*. The effective demands and supplies of goods and assets could fall to levels at which many persons, who would be willing to work for the going wage rate, are excluded from getting a job. Keynes considered such 'underemployment equilibria' to be frequent and persistent phenomena. In his view, (neo)classical full-employment equilibrium was nothing but a hypothetical ideal case.

Why wouldn't reductions in real wages automatically restore equilibrium in the labour market? Keynes had two answers to this question. First, wages are not a cost factor only, but an important element of effective demand, too. The effects of wage cuts on aggregate demand can be negative. Second, Keynes stressed that money is not neutral; it affects investment and employment through its pivotal role as the most liquid asset. No wage cuts will alter unemployment, if speculation on falling bond and stock prices increases liquidity preference. This makes interest rates rise to such levels that investment falls short of the volume required to achieve full employment. Keynes's *General Theory* led to the policy conclusion that, whenever effective demand is reduced by market forces, the emergence of underemployment can be prevented only if the government is prepared to stabilize demand by way of additional public spending.

Keynesianism

Soon after the publication of the *General Theory* people began to speak of 'the Keynesian revolution', and thirty-five years later even the president of the United States, the Republican Richard Nixon, claimed that 'we are all Keynesians now'. If there really was a revolution, it did not have quite the effects that Keynes had expected. Keynesianism split into various lines of thinking and went completely out of fashion in the 1970s and 1980s. When it came back as New Keynesianism in the 1990s, it was in rather different shapes. What had happened?

As mentioned above, Hicks (1937) had compared *Mr Keynes and the Classics* in the framework of a comparative-static model, which later was dubbed IS-LM and used in most of the macroeconomic textbooks. The basics of IS-LM are the following: I denotes investment, S saving, L the demand for money (liquidity), and M the supply of money. Investment is a function of the (real) rate of interest and saving a function of real income which equals the net domestic product. Money is held for transactions and speculative optimization of wealth. Its demand therefore depends on both income and interest. The money supply is autonomously determined by the central bank. In this way, five market equilibria can be illustrated by one figure, with the rate of interest (r) on the vertical axis and aggregate income (Y) on the horizontal axis (see Figure 8). The IS curve represents all combinations of interest and income that yield equilibria in the capital market (and indirectly in the market for consumption goods). Correspondingly, the LM curve shows all combinations of interest and income that yield equilibria in the money market (and indirectly in the bonds market as a representative market for financial assets). Macroeconomic equilibrium is then defined as that combination of interest and income at which the IS curve intersects the LM curve. Depending on the slopes and positions of the curves, IS-LM equilibrium can be a full-employment equilibrium (Y^*) or an underemployment equilibrium (Y_0).

For Hicks, IS-LM analysis served to show that both the key features of Keynes's *General Theory* and the standard approach of neoclassical economics could be captured by one and the same model. Keynes had considered his theory to be incompatible with neoclassical theory. Moreover, he claimed that it was a *general* theory, whereas the neoclassical standard model was confined to the special case of full flexibility of all prices, wages and interest rates. Hicks's synthetical model conflicted with that view, but Keynes did not protest.

IS-LM was the first step towards a combination of Keynes's ideas with neoclassical general equilibrium theory. Samuelson (1955) named it the

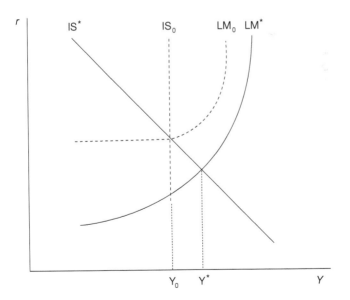

Figure 8 The IS-LM Model

neoclassical synthesis, as it presented neoclassical full-employment equilibrium as the benchmark case and reduced the theoretical domain of Keynes to three special cases in which underemployment equilibria could develop from (i) a liquidity trap, (ii) an investment trap, or (iii) from rigid wages and prices. A liquidity trap is a situation in which the interest elasticity of money demand and hence the market rate of interest are too high to be compatible with full employment; it is illustrated by the horizontal part of the LM_0 curve in Figure 8. In that situation, neither a reduction in the price level nor an autonomous increase in the money supply will lead to a lower rate of interest and higher effective demand. An investment trap (the IS_0 vertical in Figure 8) is a situation in which investment does not respond to any changes in the rate of interest. Profit expectations may be too pessimistic, and hence the marginal efficiency of capital too low, to induce sufficient investment. Both traps are best avoided by additional demand through public spending, as recommended by Keynes.

As time went by, however, the functional relationships of the IS-LM analysis were recast in terms of microtheoretical models that threw doubts on the relevance of liquidity and investment traps. Franco Modigliani (1918–2003), James Tobin (1918–2002), William Baumol (b. 1922) and Don Patinkin (1922–95), all working at different universities in the United States, were the main contributors to these 'microfoundations' of the synthesis. The traps were reduced to mere possibilities; and even if they developed, they were not likely to persist for more than a very short period. Hence, wage and price rigidities seemed to offer the last and only route to the explanation of underemployment equilibria. Such deficiencies in the downward flexibility of prices and wages did not play any central role in Keynes's *General Theory*. Yet they served well to motivate growth-oriented stabilization policies of the 1950s and 1960s that were labelled as 'Keynesian global demand management'. In general they consisted of a mix of expansionary fiscal and monetary policies, in which central banks monetized public debt by purchasing treasury bonds in order to stabilize interest rates at low levels. In this way, the volumes of money began to grow to the extent that inflation became a persistent phenomenon.

In 1960, the MIT economists Samuelson and Solow suggested that there is a trade-off between monetary stability and full employment or, in negative terms, that there is a choice to be made between inflation and unemployment. They based their argument on the so-called Phillips curve (see Figure 9).

Originally, that downward-sloped curve showed a stable, negative correlation between changes in nominal wages and the rate of unemployment, as a result of regressions which the LSE economist Alban Williams Phillips (1914–75) had run on British data. Under certain assumptions, the original Phillips curve could be interpreted to indicate a stable trade-off between

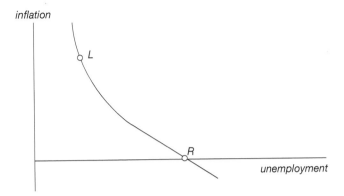

Figure 9 The (Modified) Phillips Curve

inflation and unemployment. The trade-off seemed to suggest that policy makers have to make a 'menu choice'. Either they target full employment which would not, however, come without high rates of inflation (point *L* in Figure 9), or they attempt to keep the price level stable at the cost of high unemployment (point *R*). The Phillips curve implied that money is not neutral in the long run. In the 1960s, policymakers and economists generally preferred the full-employment menu (point *L)*, since they believed that unemployment would be more costly for society than changes in the price level.

IS-LM and the Phillips curve were basic elements of the neoclassical synthesis that turned out to be the most popular interpretation of Keynes's *General Theory*. However, Keynesianism has come in greater variety. Apart from the latest version (discussed in the last section), we should mention two older ones that have been labelled 'Cambridge Keynesianism' and 'the Keynesian synthesis' (see Figure 7).

The term *Cambridge Keynesianism* is frequently applied to a group of Keynes's disciples who endeavoured to develop theories of capital, growth and distribution that fundamentally differ from the neoclassical approach. The most prominent members of that group were Roy Harrod (1900–78), Joan Robinson (1903–83), Richard Kahn (1905–89) and Nicholas Kaldor (1908–86). The Cambridge Keynesians took the position that money is 'fundamentally non-neutral' with regard to real economic activity. They argued that monetary economies are characterized by an inherent uncertainty about profits and instability of the growth process which tends to produce persistent unemployment. They pleaded for its prevention by permanent state intervention in the market process. The writings of the Cambridge Keynesians are, however, too diverse to be captured in a single core model that could be compared to IS-LM analysis.

The *Keynesian synthesis*, on the other hand, was an attempt to combine neoclassical microtheory with Keynesian macrotheory so as to emphasize the general validity of Keynes's ideas. The Israeli Patinkin, who studied and worked at the University of Chicago in the 1950s and 1960s, is one of the pioneers. His *Money, Interest and Prices* (1965) both finalized the work on the neoclassical synthesis and began the work on the Keynesian synthesis. Other important contributors are Robert Clower (1926–2011), Axel Leijonhufvud (born 1933), both then at Northwestern University in the USA, and Edmond Malinvaud (born 1923) of INSEE, the National Institute for Statistics and Economic Studies in France. The Keynesian synthesis was based on the simple trick of using Walrasian hypotheses about rational decision making, but reversing the standard assumption that prices are more flexible than quantities. Thus it was *not* assumed that market processes always generate equilibrium prices instantaneously and without costs. If price formation is a time-consuming and costly process, many transactions are likely to be carried out at 'false prices', at which markets fail to clear. In the course of such 'false trading' either sellers or buyers will be rationed, i.e. they cannot fully accomplish the sales or purchases that they have planned. If, for instance, the demand for labour falls short of supply at the going (real) wage rate, some people will become unemployed or all people will become part-time unemployed. The excess supply may lead to wage or price adjustments, but it will simultaneously affect other markets. With wage incomes being below their planned levels, consumption plans have to be revised. The decline in effective demand for consumer goods induces further cuts in the demand for labour – and so on. Prices may adjust, but not quickly enough to prevent further spillovers of rationing through the market system.

The neoclassical theory of rational decisions in perfect competition was thus transformed into a *dual decision hypothesis*. In the special case of Walrasian general equilibrium, all market agents will be able to realize their plans for supply and demand. In this case, plans depend on prices only. Alternatively, some (or all) market agents cannot fully realize their plans. They have to revise them to the extent that they produce disequilibria in other markets which in many cases feed back to the market in which rationing first occurred. In this Keynesian synthesis, Walrasian equilibrium is a purely hypothetical case. The real world is full of rationing, such as queues, waiting times and other phenomena that conflict with the assumption of fully flexible prices. The problem with the Keynesian synthesis is that it is not a general theory. It lacks the analytical tools for predicting when, how and to what extent quantity rationing will induce price adjustments.

Counter-revolutions

The counter-reaction to the 'Keynesian revolution' came in two waves. The first one – labelled as *monetarism* and originating in Chicago – rose slowly and culminated in the 1970s. The second one – labelled *new classical economics*, also originating in Chicago – followed suit and culminated in the 1980s.

Monetarism

The 'monetarist counter-revolution' began in 1956, when Milton Friedman (1912–2006) of the University of Chicago published *The Quantity Theory: A Restatement*. About twenty years later, when Friedman was awarded the Nobel Prize in Economics (in 1976) and many central banks had shifted to monetary targetry, monetarist liberalism seemed to have won out over Keynesian attempts at 'social engineering' and 'fine-tuning' of the economy. Other important contributions to the monetarist literature were made by the Canadian Harry Johnson (1923–77), professor at the LSE, Chicago and Geneva; the Swiss Karl Brunner (1916–89), professor at Rochester; and English Canadian David Laidler (b. 1938), professor at Manchester and later at Western Ontario.

Friedman's critique of Keynesianism was based on a microtheoretical reinterpretation of both Keynesian and quantity theory. He argued that the quantity theory was essentially a theory of money demand, and not merely a hypothesis about price-level determination. In the traditions of Fisher, Marshall and the early Keynes, Friedman conceptualized money demand as demand for real balances, i.e. as money holdings adjusted for inflation. Therefore money demand is codetermined by the rate of inflation and its effects on holdings of other assets. Friedman's theoretical and historical studies led to the conclusion that money demand (in terms of real balances) was much more stable than the Keynesians had claimed it to be. On the base of its stability it could be shown that the price level is determined by the quantity of money.

The decisive breakthrough for this restatement of the quantity theory was achieved by the critique of the Phillips curve that Friedman presented in his presidential address to the American Economic Association, published as 'The Role of Monetary Policy' in the *American Economic Review* in 1968. He rejected the hypothesis of a stable trade-off between inflation and unemployment, interpreting the downward-sloping Phillips curve as a short-term phenomenon that resulted from temporary 'money illusion'. Friedman postulated the existence of a 'natural rate of unemployment' that is completely independent of monetary policy.

At any moment of time, there is some level of unemployment which has the property that it is consistent with equilibrium in the structure of *real* wage rates . . . The 'natural rate of unemployment', in other words, is the level that would be ground out by the Walrasian system of general equilibrium equations, provided there is embedded in them the actual structural characteristics of the labor and commodity markets, including market imperfections, stochastic variability in demands and supplies, the cost of gathering information about job vacancies and labor availabilities, the costs of mobility, and so on.

(Friedman 1968, p. 8)

The 'natural rate of unemployment' implies that those who are without a job prefer not to work at the going (real) wage rate. Unemployment is purely voluntary, corresponding to preferences. In this situation, an expansionary fiscal and monetary policy could lower the rate of unemployment only if workers underestimate the rate of inflation and confuse nominal wage increases with a rise in real income. In that case, they tend to increase their supply of labour. Employers, on the other hand, generally have more correct expectations of inflation, as they set prices. Since inflation lowers real wages, they can cut costs, and thus profit from inflation. Hence the firms increase their demand of labour. Sooner or later, however, workers will notice that their real wages have been reduced. They will demand wage compensation, thereby reducing labour demand, or they will cut their supply of labour back to the 'natural' level.

In order to achieve full employment (in the statistical sense of employing more or less the whole labour force), the monetary authorities would have to surprise workers again and again by an acceleration of inflation. The short-term Phillips curves would become steeper, and the social costs of high inflation would obviously exceed the costs of (moderate) unemployment. Finally, high inflation would turn into hyperinflation, making prospects of long-term investment and employment extremely uncertain, against all the intentions of Keynesian stabilization policy. Friedman concluded that policymakers do not have a choice between inflation and unemployment. In the long run, the Phillips curve is a vertical line at the 'natural rate of unemployment'. By definition, that rate is compatible with any rate of inflation.

Keynesians could easily have responded that this critique was speaking at cross purposes. Friedman was discussing political manipulations aimed at reducing unemployment below the level of voluntary unemployment, whereas the Keynesians wanted to reduce involuntary unemployment. However, Friedman's message became very popular over time. His critique of demand management convinced those who were sceptical of 'social engineering'. He claimed that monetary policy works with long and variable lags, and that fiscal policy is even less reliable. Keynesian strategies of countercyclical policy would thus tend to aggravate business cycles rather than mitigate them. The stagflation of the 1970s, which could be interpreted as a big outward shift of the Phillips curve (higher inflation correlated with higher unemployment), seemed to prove Friedman right. It discredited the Keynesian approach.

Monetarism got its name from the conclusion that stabilization policy should be confined to stabilizing expectations of inflation at a low level. Monetary policy should be restored to the leading role that it had had until the 1930s. The prime task of central banks should be to keep money growth on a time path that corresponds to the growth of the economy's production potential. In this view, the free play of market forces is, in principle, fully sufficient to produce and maintain full employment.

New classical economics

In accordance with their Fisher Connection, the monetarists attempted to underpin the neutrality postulate of the neoclassical dichotomy with an analysis of market adjustments to changes in inflation. They interpreted the observable non-neutralities of money as short-run phenomena that result from the interaction of inappropriate monetary policy and 'frictions' in the market process. The frictions were mainly expressed as time lags in adjustments of expectations to actual changes in the price level. Those lags were captured by the hypothesis of adaptive expectations, which states that people form their expectations about future inflation by taking into account their earlier errors.

The adaptive expectations hypothesis soon came under attack by new classical critics. Robert Lucas (b. 1937), another Chicago professor who was awarded the Nobel Prize (in 1995), and Thomas Sargent (b. 1940) of the University of Minnesota demanded that all economic theory must be firmly based on the rigorous microfoundations of Walrasian general equilibrium theory. All changes in the levels of production and employment should be explained as results of rational behaviour under the assumptions of full price flexibility and continuous market clearing. The new classical micro-foundations are incompatible with the concepts of involuntary unemployment and adaptive expectations. In their framework, all unemployment is the result of intertemporal optimization of consumption and leisure. Consequently, the new classical economists adopted the monetarist concept of a natural rate of unemployment. On the other hand, they considered adaptive expectations to be inconsistent with rational behaviour, as they are backward-looking and systematically erroneous in the sense that they can lead to permanent under- or overestimation of inflation. Since market agents are assumed to maximize utility or profit, they will make use of all accessible information about future developments in markets and in economic policy. Their expectations are forward-looking and rational in the sense that all systematic errors will be eliminated in the search for utility and profit gains.

Given these assumptions, only a completely erratic, unpredictable type of monetary policy could be non-neutral with regard to unemployment. A 'stabilization policy' that strives to shock markets into reducing unemployment cannot be rational even from a Keynesian point of view. It would destabilize the economy by creating additional uncertainty and would therefore not live up to its name. Hence, the new classical insistence on rational expectations corroborates the monetarist critique of the Phillips curve trade-off. It actually does more than that. It takes the critique to the radical conclusion that the trade-off does not even exist in the short run.

Lucas attempted to explain business cycles as responses to monetary shocks, i.e. as changes in aggregate supply in reaction to unforeseeable inflationary impulses that are confused with changes in relative prices. Even this last vestige of non-neutrality of money was eliminated by the next round of new classical economics. This came under the label of *real business cycle* or RBC theory and was led by Edward Prescott (b. 1940) and the Norwegian Finn Kydland (b. 1943), both then at Carnegie-Mellon University at Pittsburgh, USA and Nobel Prize winners of 2004. In their paper *Time to Build and Aggregate Fluctuations* (1982), Prescott and Kydland took the Walrasian imperative seriously, of explaining observed fluctuations of macroeconomic variables exclusively from changes in the fundamental data of tastes and technology. They and other RBC theorists modelled business cycles as optimal responses to technology shocks and unforeseeable shifts in preferences. In the RBC approach money is completely neutral, irrelevant for the explanation of changes in production and employment.

New syntheses?

With this brief account of the development of monetary macroeconomics up to the 1970s we seem to have come back full circle to the (neo)classical dichotomy. But the controversies about the neutrality of money did not end then and there.

New Keynesians

Many economists felt provoked by the new classical tenets of fully flexible prices, continuous market clearing and, in particular, by the corollary view that involuntary unemployment is not a meaningful concept. Attempting to restore this notion, which seems to have some correspondence in reality, as well as other Keynesian ideas to theoretical respectability, the new Keynesians have, to some extent, gone along with the new classical demands for rigorous microfoundations. Their approaches have been inspired particularly by the works of the two Nobel Prize winners George Akerlof (b. 1940) of the University of California at Berkeley, and Joseph Stiglitz (b. 1943), who in the relevant years worked at the universities of Yale, Oxford and Stanford. Akerlof and Stiglitz underpinned the traditional Keynesian arguments about quantity rationing and price rigidities with theories about rational behaviour in the presence of asymmetrically distributed information and the power to set prices (imperfect competition). If, for instance, employers cannot at a reasonable cost monitor the work efforts of their employees *ex ante*, they may use wage increases and wage differentiation as incentives to raise productivity. Under plausible assumptions, such profit-maximizing 'efficiency wage setting' can generate a downward rigidity of wages that is fully compatible with the existence of involuntary unemployment.

Apart from efficiency wages, New Keynesians explain underemployment equilibria with price adjustment costs or credit rationing that arises from information asymmetries between borrowers and lenders. Cuts in productive capacity and employment can, within a short time, destroy capital that takes a long time to rebuild. New Keynesians emphasize this asymmetry with regard to real capital (industrial plants etc.), 'human capital' (qualifications) and 'information capital' (trust and confidence). They argue that restrictive monetary policy can contribute to the destruction of capital and, consequently, to the rise and persistence of unemployment. From a new Keynesian point of view, there is a trade-off between employment and *dis*inflation (a lowering of inflation rates), which bears a certain resemblance to the old Phillips curve.

The new neoclassical synthesis

In a nutshell, the dialectics of macroeconomics may be summarized as follows: Keynes proclaimed his *General Theory* to be the antithesis of (neo-classical) economics, but before long the Keynesian Revolution was turned into the neoclassical synthesis. Even so it provoked monetarist and new classical counter-revolutions, which culminated in real business cycle theory. The new Keynesian reaction to these challenges has led to the development of the *new neoclassical synthesis* – which is where the (hi)story ends for now.

By analogy with the IS-LM model of the old neoclassical synthesis, the new synthesis is described as IS-AS-MP, a three-equations system through which output (gaps), inflation and interest are jointly determined. An intertemporal IS relation is usually combined with an aggregate-supply function in terms of a new Keynesian Phillips curve, and a reaction function for monetary policy, typically in the form of a Taylor rule for setting interest rates. This triad is, in some version or other, at the centre of current mainstream macroeconomics and has begun to make its way into the textbooks. The most influential contribution so far was made by Michael Woodford, then at Princeton University, under the title *Interest and Prices: Foundations of a Theory of Monetary Policy* (2003). Both the title and the book's core chapters refer back beyond Keynes, to Wicksell's *Geldzins und Güterpreise* (1898). The basic IS-AS-Taylor model that Woodford develops for his extensive analysis of monetary policy is described as 'neo-Wicksellian framework'.

Woodford has chosen Wicksell as patron saint for his version of the new synthesis, because he, like Wicksell, shifts the focus of monetary policy from the volume of money to the relationship between the actual interest rate and a 'natural rate'. Moreover, his discussion of the monetary policy function has much in common with Wicksell's proposal to eliminate inflation by adjusting nominal interest rates to changes in the price level. Moreover, by referring to the Wicksellians of the 1920s and 1930s (in particular Hayek, Lindahl and Myrdal), Woodford grounds his advocacy of inflation control on the potential non-neutrality of monetary policy: '[I]t is because instability of the general level of prices causes substantial real distortions – leading to inefficient variation both in aggregate employment and output and in the sectoral composition of economic activity – that price stability is important' (2003, p. 5).

Yet the new neoclassical synthesis does not only have a Wicksell Connection. It also has an obvious Fisher Connection. The IS function represents the intertemporal optimization of a representative agent in Fisherian terms, including the distinction between nominal and real interest rates. In this setting of continuous equilibrium of investment and saving, it is not quite straightforward to model coordination failures of the interest-rate mechanism, and references to the old bone of contention, the neutrality of money, are carefully avoided. The new synthesis is probably not the last word on the core issues of macroeconomics. Further (counter-)revolutions may be attempted. However, it is often only the style of the arguments that changes, while much of their contents would have been well understood by the middle of the twentieth century, if not earlier.

References

Boianovsky, Mauro and Trautwein, Hans-Michael (2006a) Haberler, the League of Nations, and the Quest for Consensus in Business Cycle Theory in the 1930s, *History of Political Economy* 38: 45–89.

Boianovsky, Mauro and Trautwein, Hans-Michael (2006b) Wicksell after Woodford, *Journal of the History of Economic Thought* 28: 171–85.

Fisher, Irving (1911) *The Purchasing Power of Money: Its Determination and Relation to Credit, Interest and Prices.* New York: Macmillan.

Fisher, Irving (1933) The Debt-Deflation Theory of Great Depressions, *Econometrica* 1: 337–59.

Friedman, Milton (1969) *The Optimum Quantity of Money and Other Essays.* London: Macmillan.

Friedman, Milton (1987) The Quantity Theory of Money. *The New Palgrave: A Dictionary of Economics.* London: Macmillan.

Jonung, Lars (1991, ed.) *The Stockholm School of Economics Revisited.* Cambridge: Cambridge University Press.

Keynes, John Maynard (1973) [1936] *The General Theory of Employment, Interest and Money*, vol. VII of the *Collected Writings of John Maynard Keynes.* London: Macmillan.

Laidler, David (1999) *Fabricating the Keynesian Revolution: Studies of the Inter-War Literature on Money, the Cycle, and Unemployment.* Cambridge: Cambridge University Press.

Leijonhufvud, Axel (1981) The Wicksell Connection: Variations on a Theme. In *Information and Coordination: Essays in Macroeconomic Theory.* Oxford: Oxford University Press.

Lindahl, Erik (1939) *Studies in the Theory of Money and Capital.* London: George Allen & Unwin.

Lucas, Robert (1987) *Models of Business Cycles.* Oxford: Basil Blackwell.

Lucas, Robert (1996) Nobel Lecture – Monetary Neutrality, *Journal of Political Economy* 104: 661–82.

Myrdal, Gunnar (1939) [1931] *Monetary Equilibrium.* London: William Hodge.

Patinkin, Don (1965) *Money, Interest and Prices*, 2nd ed. New York: Harper and Row.

Samuelson, Paul (1955) *Economics: An Introductory Analysis.* New York: McGraw-Hill.

Snowdon, Brian and Vane, Howard (2005) *Modern Macroeconomics: Its Origins, Development and Current State.* Cheltenham: Edward Elgar.

Tobin, James (1987) Irving Fisher. *The New Palgrave: A Dictionary of Economics.* London: Macmillan.

Wicksell, Knut (1936) [1898] *Interest and Prices: A Study of the Causes Regulating the Value of Money.* London: Macmillan.

Woodford, Michael (2003) *Interest and Prices: Foundations of a Theory of Monetary Policy.* Princeton, NJ: Princeton University Press.

7   Orthodoxy and change

The famous author George Bernard Shaw (who was also a member of the Fabian Society and co-founder of the London School of Economics) once quipped that, if all economists were laid end to end, they would not reach a conclusion. As should be obvious from the preceding chapters, the history of economic thought is indeed a controversial and open-ended affair. Instead of a conclusion we will therefore, at the end of the book, offer brief surveys, first of the current orthodoxy and heterodox approaches, then of theories about scientific progress, and finally of other useful guides through the history of economic thought.

Orthodox and heterodox economics

The preceding chapters have shown that the views on economic problems have varied over time. Almost all of the time, different schools have co-existed, often with one school dominating. By definition, the dominating school is considered as *orthodoxy*, i.e. as correct doctrine, by the majority of contemporaneous economists. Other approaches, at variance with the dominating school, are called *heterodox*; their followers, too, do of course consider them as correct. We hope that we have been able to show that there is no easy way to say which school is 'the correct one'. Different schools emphasize different aspects and may be 'right' or 'wrong' in different respects. Ideas that are regarded as results of best research practice at one point in time may be considered misleading soon thereafter, but make a comeback later. The varying opinions on the quantity theory of money or on policies to maximize social wealth and welfare may serve as examples. Therefore, a combination of respect for, and criticism of, different opinions is an advisable attitude for a serious economist.

Current orthodoxy and its extensions

Neoclassical economics is undoubtedly the current orthodoxy. At present, a large majority of economists holds the belief that utility maximization and market equilibrium are key concepts of analysis. Most of the research literature is based on them in one way or other. But stating that neoclassical economics is orthodoxy does not amount to much, as it comes in so many varieties that hardly anyone thinks of it as a well-defined school. It is rather seen as a general toolkit, out of which economists in one field select one set of analytical instruments for their purposes, while those in other fields pick other sets.

The 'toolkit' metaphor is frequently used by those who have extended the application of neoclassical methods beyond the traditional core areas of general equilibrium theory and welfare economics. Various labels, such as *new political economy* and *new institutional economics*, indicate that issues that used to be in the domain of other schools are now tackled with neoclassical methods. Employing the marginal principle and some concept of market equilibrium, politics and even law are analysed as processes of rent distribution linked with politicians' utility maximization. *Public Choice* is another common label of this direction. This is quite different from classical political economy and earlier neoclassicists who often assumed the economy to be ruled by some benevolent dictator; and it seems to be more realistic. Contrary to the views of the historical and institutionalist schools, the emergence of institutions is now frequently explained in terms of individual maximizing behaviour, with the minimization of transaction costs as the specific marginal principle to apply. Key contributions to both lines of research have been made by Mancur Olson (1932–98), while at Princeton; by Oliver Williamson (b. 1932), the Nobel Prize winner of 2009, while at the University of Pennsylvania; by James Buchanan (1919–2013), Nobel Prize winner of 1986, and Gordon Tullock (b. 1922); and by the economic historian and Nobel Prize winner of 1993, Douglass North (b. 1920), while at the University of Washington.

The neoclassical principles of rational economic behaviour have been so universally applied that there has been talk about 'economic imperialism'. Many economists analyse supposedly 'non-economic subjects', such as art, marriage and drug addiction, with neoclassical tools. The Chicago economist and Nobel Prize winner of 1992, Gary Becker (b. 1930) is the most frequently mentioned pioneer in this particular branch.

However, the extensions of neoclassical analysis may also imply modifications of the theoretical core. The conventional constructions of the *homo oeconomicus* of the microeconomic textbooks and the so-called microfoundations of macroeconomics have come under fire wherever advanced methods of other disciplines, such as mathematics, biology and psychology, are employed. It is open to debate as to how far the new lines of research in game theory, behavioural and experimental economics are still 'genuinely' neo-classical in character or may have started to overturn the present orthodoxy.

Before we turn to these new lines, we will take a look at the outright anti-neoclassical approaches of the most prominent heterodox schools. A considerable number of economists work on the premise that obeying the first principles of neoclassical economics in all matters of economic research would require them to make dubious shortcuts or inefficiently roundabout arguments. Or they deem those principles to be simply wrong.

Heterodox schools

One of the oldest heterodox schools is *neo-Ricardianism*, which was discussed at the ends of Chapters 3 and 4. It is a school that might have been considered orthodox in the nineteenth century, but is now heterodox, i.e. at variance with the core of neoclassical economics. Core contributions to the neo-Ricardian critique of neoclassical economics are found, for example, in Piero Sraffa's comments on Alfred Marshall's industrial economics in the 1920s, and in the capital controversies of the two Cambridges (see Chapter 4).

In the capital controversies, neo-Ricardianism worked in alliance with Cambridge Keynesianism (see Chapter 6). Joan Robinson, Nicolas Kaldor and other members of the latter group became patron saints of *Post Keynesianism*, another heterodox school, whose deepest roots reach back beyond Keynes to Malthus, Ricardo and Marx. The influence of Marx on Post Keynesianism has largely been transmitted via the Polish Cambridge economist Michal Kalecki (1899–1970). Using a Marxist frame of reference, Kalecki distinguished between workers and capitalists. Like Keynes he concluded that unemployment is an inherent property of the capitalist economy, that the latter exhibits cyclical fluctuations, and that the price mechanism is unable to eliminate the problems. Following the *financial instability hypothesis* of Hyman Minsky (1919–96), who was a student of Schumpeter at Harvard and later professor at Washington University in St. Louis, Post Keynesians also stress the links between speculation, instability and liquidity preference in monetary economies. They usually plead for comprehensive and coordinated state intervention to stabilize effective demand and employment.

At the other end of the political spectrum we find *Modern Austrian Economics*. This is another heterodoxy with roots in earlier orthodoxy, in the teachings of Menger and his followers (see Chapter 4). Modern Austrians (who are not required to be citizens of Austria) would usually reject the classification of Menger, Böhm-Bawerk and Wieser as neoclassical economists. Mises and Hayek, the founding fathers of the school (who also figured in Chapter 6), strongly criticized neoclassical economics for its deterministic equilibrium analysis and implicit support of state interventionism. Modern Austrians are radical subjectivists and libertarians. They regard a system of free markets primarily as a necessary condition for the freedom of the individual, and not primarily as an efficient device for solving problems of resource allocation (as in neoclassical economics). In their concepts of market processes, innovative entrepreneurs are the driving forces of economic development, due to their propensity to take commercial risks. Because such action is based on purely subjective judgments, Modern Austrians tend to reject the use of mathematical models and econometric methods. (They should therefore not be confused with 'neo-Austrian' approaches to capital theory that, in the traditions of Böhm-Bawerk, Wicksell and Hicks, attempt to elucidate the role of time in capital formation by way of rather complex modelling.)

The ideas of Joseph Schumpeter (1883–1950) about the role of the entrepreneur were such that (apart from his original citizenship) he too could be considered a Modern Austrian. Yet Schumpeter, whom we have mentioned occasionally in earlier chapters, does not easily fit any pattern. He was both ortho- and heterodox, admiring Marx and Walras, and creating his own *Theory of Economic Development* (1911), in which development is described as a process of 'creative destruction', as cyclical growth that is driven by innovation and imitation.

Schumpeter is now a key figure of *evolutionary economics*, which is sometimes labelled as *neo-Schumpeterian economics*. This rather loose grouping of economists could, true to the nature of their patron saint, be considered as heterodox from some angles, and as orthodox from others. Evolutionary economics overlaps with institutional economics, but puts greater emphasis on innovation and the diffusion of knowledge and technologies. The role of history and path dependence in economic development is stressed to a greater extent than in standard neoclassical growth theory or development economics.

In recent years, however, the mainstream literature on economic growth and development has turned into an evolutionary direction, developing a much greater awareness of path dependence and the importance of innovation and institutions. The work of the MIT economist Daron Acemoglu (b. 1967) and his co-authors may serve as examples. Similarly, the new institutional economics has taken an evolutionary turn in the works of Douglass North and co-authors after 1989.

New methods

Since the middle of the twentieth century, neoclassical economics has also been challenged and transformed by a number of new methods. Game theory, behavioural economics and experimental economics are examples that may now be considered part of mainstream economics, and the foremost representatives have been awarded a Nobel Prize. Game theory models strategic interaction, i.e. the behaviour of two or more decision makers whose decisions influence each other. Modern game theory has developed since the 1940s, but one may find references as far back as the eighteenth century. The Hungarian John von Neumann (1903–57) and the Austrian Oskar Morgenstern (1902–77), who both emigrated to the United States in the 1930s and worked at Princeton University, laid the foundations with their *Theory of Games and Economic Behaviour* (1944).

As time went on, two main versions of game theory developed. One deals with cooperative games, where coalitions are important and agreements, promises and threats are binding and enforceable. The other focuses on non-cooperative games and is the version that has dominated research in recent decades. John Harsanyi (1920–2000) of the University of California at Berkeley, John Nash (b. 1928) of Princeton and Reinhard Selten (b. 1930) of Bonn have made important contributions and were jointly awarded the Nobel Prize in 1994. While game theory in both versions can be used to reproduce central results of Walrasian general equilibrium theory, it has also exposed the fact that these results are based on a host of very specific assumptions. Other, a priori equally plausible, models of market processes lead to completely different results.

In the works of main figures like Smith, Marshall and Keynes, there is much reasoning about the complicated nature of the human mind. However, much economic theorizing has been built on a simplified creature, *homo oeconomicus* or economic man, who is a completely selfish, fully informed and utility-maximizing robot driven primarily by material incentives. *Behavioural economics* is a branch that introduces more realistic features of psychology. Early works include contributions in the 1950s by Maurice Allais (1911–2010) of Paris and Herbert Simon (1916–2001) of Carnegie-Mellon University, Pittsburgh. In the 1970s, the psychologists Daniel Kahneman (b. 1934) and Amos Tversky (1937–1996), both of the Hebrew University of Jerusalem, introduced cognitive psychology into economics. Simon, Allais and Kahneman were awarded the Nobel Prize in economics in 1978, 1988 and 2002, respectively.

One important result of behavioural economics is that people are often unable to analyse situations which involve probability calculations. They often draw too far-reaching conclusions from small samples. A simple example is the gambler's fallacy: If three tosses of a fair coin give heads, many individuals erroneously believe that the probability that the fourth toss will give a tail is larger than fifty per cent. Another result is that decision making under risk often diverges from predictions of expected utility theory, a core concept of standard neoclassical economics. Kahneman and Tversky proposed a *prospect theory*, which is built on empirical observations rather than on seemingly attractive axioms. Much research in behavioural economics is done on financial markets and various (other) types of addictive behaviour.

Based on the assumption that people weigh private benefits against private costs, neglecting the impact on others, it is sometimes suggested that individual ownership or government regulations are more efficient ways than common ownership to economize on resources like fish stocks, pastures, woods, lakes and ground water basins. However, Elinor Ostrom (1933–2012), Nobel prize winner in 2009 (together with Oliver Williamson), has found that common property is often surprisingly well managed. Users themselves can both create and enforce rules that mitigate overexploitation, which standard elementary theory of economic behaviour would hardly predict.

Sometimes the behaviour of economic actors can be illustrated by economic experiments. For a long time economics had been considered a non-experimental discipline which had to rely only on field data or the lessons of history. This view was challenged in the mid-twentieth century, when experimental economic studies were started to be made in laboratory settings. A major protagonist of this development is Vernon Smith (b. 1927), who then worked at the University of Arizona. Smith shared the Nobel Prize (in 2002) with Kahneman – a fact that indicates the close connection between behavioural economics and experimental economics.

In experimental economics, human behaviour is studied in situations that imitate the market – for example in different forms of auctions. Some of those forms are actually used on international commodity markets or when public monopolies are deregulated and privatized.

Theories about the development of theories

Besides philosophical discussions about the essence of science, especially about the distinction between science and non-science (where the readiness to give a definite answer has diminished), a number of theories have been presented about the driving forces behind the development of a discipline. Here we present different views held among economists, that range from the belief in a cumulative growth of our knowledge directed by unselfish truth-seeking to the opinion that persuasive powers and belief in authority are decisive.

Scientific revolutions

In 1962 the American Thomas Kuhn (1922–96), then working at Berkeley, published his book *The Structure of Scientific Revolutions*. Kuhn was originally a physicist and had the natural sciences in mind when he presented his ideas about scientific revolutions. During normal circumstances, scientific problems are resolved within the framework of a generally accepted 'paradigm', which Kuhn defined as 'the entire constellation of beliefs, values, techniques, and so on shared by the members of a given community'. However, as time goes by, it becomes apparent that more and more questions cannot be answered within the given paradigm. A crisis appears that may pave the way for a new paradigm.

> Because it demands large-scale paradigm destruction and major shifts in the problems and techniques of normal science, the emergence of new theories is generally preceded by a period of pronounced professional insecurity. As one might expect, that insecurity is generated by the persistent failure of the puzzles of normal science to come out as they should. Failure of existing rules is the prelude to a search for new ones.
> (Kuhn 1962, pp. 67–8)

If the crisis is severe enough, and if there is no alternative paradigm which gives an answer to the questions that the former could not answer, the new paradigm may be accepted and replace the old one. A scientific revolution is taking place. The revolution does not always and in every respect imply progress. 'There are losses as well as gains in scientific revolutions, and scientists tend to be peculiarly blind to the former' (Kuhn 1962, p. 167).

Kuhn himself did not like the fact that his theory was also applied to the social sciences, but this occurred nevertheless. In economic thinking, one might talk about a mercantilistic revolution that replaced scholastic thinking, physiocratic and classical revolutions that superseded mercantilism, a neoclassical revolution, a Keynesian revolution, etc. (see also Chapter 6). One objection that has been raised is that, in economics, new ideas often co-exist with old ones. The changes that have occurred are less revolutionary and meant a less complete break with earlier thought than, for example, Copernicus's heliocentric theory in astronomy, or the abandonment of the phlogiston theory in chemistry.

Lakatos's scientific research programme

Influenced by the philosopher Karl Popper and critical of Kuhn's theory, the Hungarian mathematician Imre Lakatos (1922–74), then working at the London School of Economics, presented his ideas about *Falsification and the Methodology of Scientific Research Programmes* in 1970. A research programme contains a number of theories and methodological rules. Some rules dictate which paths of research to avoid (negative heuristics), others which to pursue (positive heuristics). All research programmes are characterised by a 'hard core'. The negative heuristics forbid the scientist to question that core. Instead, auxiliary hypotheses are articulated, and they form a protective belt around the hard core. The belt of auxiliary hypotheses has to bear the brunt of attacks from outside. It may be modified or even replaced in order to defend the hard core, which may thereby become even harder. A research programme is successful if it leads to a 'progressive problem shift', i.e. if the theories of the programme make it possible to discover and predict new facts. According to Lakatos, science develops more continuously and with less dramatic changes than is claimed by Kuhn's theory of paradigm shifts.

Like Kuhn, Lakatos had applications to the natural sciences particularly in mind, but his ideas were soon adopted by social scientists. Remenyi (1979) has provided an application to neoclassical economics. According to him, the hard core of the dominant economic research programme includes the following propositions: (1) Consumers and producers can legitimately be assumed to be rational decision makers who know what they want. (2) Economic activity is motivated by individual self-interest. (3) More is better than less. (4) Given perfect knowledge and good government, economic welfare is maximized by free competition. (5) Although welfare and economic welfare are not synonymous, the latter is a good approximation for the former. (6) Stable and Pareto-efficient equilibrium solutions can be defined for any and all markets relevant to economic research and analysis. (7) Everything has its opportunity cost. (8) Abstract reduced-form models and simplifying assumptions are valid tools of economic analysis.

In addition, Remenyi adds a number of propositions under positive and negative heuristics. The positive heuristics include, among other things: Identify the relevant supply and demand functions and specify the parameters for each. Prove theorems wherever possible. If the model can be tested empirically, test it. Institutional and environmental changes that remove market imperfections will always be found to produce an increase in allocative efficiency and economic welfare.

The negative heuristics include the following propositions: Do not search for suboptimal solutions to the economic problem. Irrationality is not a legitimate behavioural assumption; economic efficiency demands rational judgment. Any problem to which supply and demand notions cannot be applied or for which supply and demand are simultaneously perfectly inelastic over time are not relevant to economic analysis.

As we have seen in the previous sections, neither these nor other applications of Lakatos's theory to economic problems are immune to objections. Even if the idea of a hard core is accepted, it is not self-evident what should be included in the hard core. Nor is it evident how a research programme is to be defined. Is the whole neoclassical complex to be regarded as a research programme, as in the example above, or does such a programme consist of a smaller part, for example trade theory or industrial economics? It is also interesting to note that Lakatos seems to give a better explanation of the inertia and obstacles to changes in research programmes than of the changes that really take place.

The rhetoric of economics

In a well-known article from 1983 with the title *The Rhetoric of Economics*, Donald (now Deirdre) McCloskey (b. 1942) investigated what determines which economic ideas will take root. According to McCloskey, there are two different attitudes to scientific method among economists, one official and the other unofficial. Officially the economist professes the Scientific Method. 'Its leading idea is that all sure knowledge is modeled on the early twentieth century's understanding of certain pieces of nineteenth century physics' (McCloskey 1983, p. 484), and it now has only limited support among philosophers of science. Because it is predominant among modern economists, McCloskey labels it 'modernism'.

The unofficial method is more implicit and becomes apparent in the actual research and in the scholar's attitude towards different questions. 'Any economist believes more than his evidence of a suitably modernist and objective sort implies' (McCloskey 1983, p. 493). McCloskey gives examples from an inquiry among economists about such things as the effect of tariffs on general economic welfare, and the effect of a ceiling on rents upon the quantity and quality of housing. The answers indicated that economists were disposed to *take it for granted* that the economy had certain characteristics. It is not necessarily wrong to do so, but it shows that economists in reality draw more far-reaching conclusions than their official method would permit.

McCloskey also shows that, even in more technical analyses, beliefs outside the official method play an important role. His conclusion is not that these kinds of beliefs, or arguments, or rhetoric should be repudiated in research, but that they should be brought to light and investigated with literary critical methods. McCloskey's attitude is reminiscent of Myrdal's insistence that researchers should explicitly report their values (see Chapter 5).

Other histories of economic thought

We cannot deny that our short history of economic thinking has also been influenced by our own values and beliefs. Even though we have tried to give a balanced overview that contains the most important ideas, we had to be selective and stress a few points while omitting others. This is perhaps most obvious from the maps at the beginning of each chapter, where we have attempted to illustrate the connections and controversies between different thinkers and schools and the evolution of concepts over time with a few labels and lines. Other historians of economic thought draw different lines and tell different stories, at least to some extent. As is obvious from the references at the end of each chapter, we have made use of others' histories, and we should end our little guide by commenting on a few of these useful sources of information, most of which are fatter books and provide considerably more detail.

It should be noted that we confine ourselves to a very small selection of references, each representing a different genre and limited to material in English language. Many more textbooks and other sources exist, and there are brilliant histories of economics in other languages, with different cultural perspectives. The Spanish, French, Japanese, German and Italian language areas, in particular, are not only large, they are also rich in traditions of economic thinking and in literature on the history of economic thought.

A classic worth reading, especially for its richness of detail and inclusion of literature from many different language areas, is Schumpeter's *History of Economic Analysis* (1954). This unfinished work of roughly 1,200 pages (in small print) is an excellent account of the developments up to the middle of the twentieth century. In addition to the presentation of the schools and thinkers and the critical examination of their ideas, Schumpeter also provides valuable reflections on 'real history' and methods of analysis.

Another classic is Mark Blaug's *Economic Theory in Retrospect* (1st ed. 1962, 5th ed. 1997), about 750 pages and including many helpful diagrams full of sharp and witty exercises of analytical reconstruction. The strength of the book is in the parts on classical political economy – not for nothing did Blaug dedicate the book 'to my son, David Ricardo'.

There are numerous histories of special fields of economics. A good example for the field of macroeconomics is *Modern Macroeconomics: Its Origins, Development and Current State* (2005) by Brian Snowdon and Howard Vane. In addition to a guide through the different schools and lines of research, the roughly 800 pages of the book contain interesting interviews with main protagonists and a comprehensive bibliography of the relevant literature.

A historically oriented encyclopaedia with valuable entries on thinkers, schools and concepts is *The New Palgrave Dictionary of Economics* (2008, also available online). An encyclopaedic source on the internet is the *History of Economic Thought Website*, formerly of the New School for Social Research, New York (now moved to a URL of the Delhi University Library System). Even though it is incomplete and apparently no longer updated, it contains useful personal entries and essays on schools of thought.

Another species is the 'reader'. For those who do not have direct access to the original texts, a collection of the most relevant passages with introductory comments may be helpful. A representative reader with a broad coverage on some 660 pages is *The History of Economic Thought: A Reader* (2003), edited by Steven Medema and Warren Samuels.

It should be noted, though, that for those who are seriously interested in studying economic theories, old or new, nothing can substitute for the experience of reading (and trying to make sense of) the original works.

References

Blaug, Mark (1997) *Economic Theory in Retrospect*, 5th ed. Cambridge: Cambridge University Press.

Kuhn, Thomas S. (1970) *The Structure of Scientific Revolutions* (2nd ed.). Chicago, IL: University of Chicago Press.

Lakatos, Imre (1970) Falsification and the Methodology of Scientific Research Programmes. In Lakatos, Imre and Musgrave, Alan (eds), *Criticism and the Growth of Knowledge*. Cambridge: Cambridge University Press.

McCloskey, Donald N. (1983) The Rhetoric of Economics. *Journal of Economic Literature* 21: 481–517.

Medema, Steven and Samuels, Warren (eds) (2003) *The History of Economic Thought: A Reader*. London: Routledge.

Remenyi, Joseph (1979) Core Demi-Core Interaction: Toward a General Theory of Disciplinary and Subdisciplinary Growth, *History of Political Economy* 11: 30–63.

Schumpeter, Joseph A. (1954) *History of Economic Analysis*. Oxford: Oxford University Press.

Snowdon, Brian and Vane, Howard (2005) *Modern Macroeconomics: Its Origins, Development and Current State*. Cheltenham: Edward Elgar.

The New Palgrave Dictionary of Economics (2008) 8 vols., ed. by Durlauf, Steven N. and Blume, Lawrence E. London: Palgrave Macmillan.

Index

Note: page numbers in *italic* refer to figures and tables

Made in the USA
San Bernardino, CA
25 August 2017